Table of Content

Dedication

I dedicate this book to my loving mother and father for their unconditional love and patience.

Leprechaun Wine

When leprechauns dine,
they sip on the finest of wine.
From the forests and glens,
they gather berries of every kind.
They blend them together
for a taste that is so unique.
Don't try to copy
their winemaking skills,
for it's a secret to them,
it's a leprechaun blend.
They don't sell it or promote it.
But if you meet one of these wee fellows,
they will give you a sip,
and they will smile at you
the moment this fine wine
touches your lips.

Real Irish Soda Bread

My aunt Florence
made Irish soda bread
the old times way.

Over a peat fire
hung a large cast iron pot.
Hot peat would be
burning underneath,
and on top of the lid
she would place
hot coals of peat
that helped the bread
to evenly bake.

Buttermilk from the farm,
flour, baking soda, salt,
also raisins and caraway seed
could be added.

The peat gave the soda bread
a unique flavor.
While it was still hot,
you spread lots of
homemade country butter.

Then there was griddle soda bread,
baked on top of a wood or coal stove.
This soda bread was also good,
and it was about
one inch and a half thick.

Soda bread baked today
in an electric or gas stove
just doesn't have the same taste

as what old fashioned soda bread had.
It's still good,
but nothing in comparison.

Needs not Greed

There are basic things
we need to survive;
clean water, food, clothing
and shelter as well.

You don't need thirty pairs
of shoes in your closet;
a different pair of pants to wear
everyday of the month;
three cars or a mansion
on top of a mountain
or a luxury home
on the beach.

There are no pockets
in shrouds
to keep your wealth in.
The world's monetary system
is not accepted up there.

People go out to eat
at a steakhouse,
and when you look at the waiter,
carrying the dinner plate
to one's table,
it looks like
there's half a cow
on the plate.
A smaller amount
would meet their
daily protein needs.

There is a vast difference
between one's needs and greeds,

and who cares about prestige?
All we need in life
is to be healthy,
and to have family values,
and thank God
for supplying our needs,
not our greeds.

We the Irish

Full of emotion
until logic sets in;
that is a fact.

Trying to reason things out,
we can get on the wrong track.
Divided we are
in so many ways,
in issues like politics
we can't seem to resolve.

Some Irish believe
the north should be ruled
by the crown,
others do not.

With a mix of
religious intolerance,
and trumped up fears,
our land is divided
from the north
to the south.

Independence from English rule
can't be resolved
with bullets and bombs,
for this is insane.

With a spin,
Irish history is taught
in some northern schools,
and not true to facts.
Some teach that
Cromwell was an English hero.

But a villain he was:
He tried to destroy Irish culture
with cannons and swords.

Let the past be gone,
and our emotions
come under control,
for we are a proud Celtic people,
as well you know.

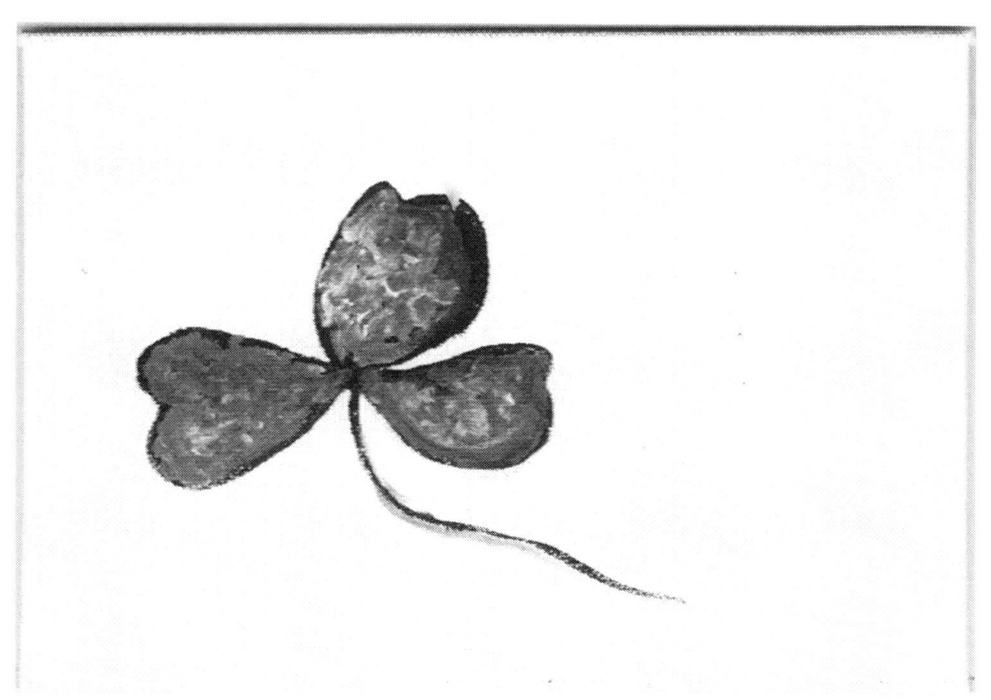

Fifty Shades of Green

The blending of the greens
with yellow, purple, red
and pink and orange.
It's Ireland's tapestry of nature
no doubt.

Wild primroses
or a green grassy slope.
Against the green,
the soft yellow
can make one mellow.

Heather in the peat bogs,
a mantel of soft purple
with dark green grass
growing in between.

The gray smoke
from an Irish cottage
on a soft green glen,
mingled with soft Irish mist,
makes one feel so warm,
and so alive.

The dark green
holly branch with berries,
red against a mantle
of snow upon the ground.
It's perfect at Irish Christmas time.

Let us not take for granted
Ireland's fifty shades of green
blended with purple, white, red and yellow.
Through God

nature has blended together.

Rich

You can be rich on earth
without silver or gold.
Love, joy, peace
will make rich
in your soul.

Gold can't buy
favor with God
up above.
But trusting in him
will bring peace
like a dove.

If you want to be
rich in your soul
do things that
please the Lord
like helping your neighbor
when he is in need,
comforting the sick,
or donating your time.
Earthly riches,
you won't have.
But one day
with the Lord
you will dine.

PEACE JOY
LOVE

Too Much

Too much
rain in early spring,
a bad potato crop
it will bring.

Too much
sleet in early May,
and the budding apple blossoms
will disappear,
and no crisp cider
the following year.

Too much
Irish soda bread and stout
will make your stomach
stick way out.

Too much
greasy Irish stew,
and your days on earth
will be a few.

Too much
watching national sports
on TV
and a couch potato
you will be.
To this
your spouse
will agree.

Too much
watching politicians
on TV,

you will become brainwashed
don't you see?

Too much
fishing or playing golf,
will make your happy
home life disappear,
and your angry spouse,
you will have to fear.

Irish Heather

Along the glens
and in the dark peat bogs,
you blossom in the spring.
Above your purple canopy,
birds of every kind
begin to sing.

The honey bee removes
a sweet nectar
from your flowers,
and within their comb,
you will find a honey
so sweet,
so rare.

There's nothing
in the world
to equal or compare.
The surface peat absorbs
your hardy roots
that grow deep below.

To avoid damage
from cold winter ice or snow,
when black peat is burned
in an open cottage fire
Your dry roots
perfume the air
beyond desire.

May Irish heather
always grow
in the peat bogs
and rugged glens,
and to the heavens

your aroma sends.

Tomorrow

There will always be a tomorrow,
God's word has told us so.
Your tomorrow could be in heaven,
not here on earth below.

Tomorrow here on earth could be
filled with strife and pain.
In the heavenly tomorrow,
there will be no strife,
or family fights,
or bills to pay.

Be ready for
a heavenly tomorrow
in case this earthly one
doesn't come.

There will be a bright tomorrow
I have trust in God
and Jesus Christ,
his son.

SYD M^c SHANE

Fairy Hill

In west County Down,
a hill is famous,
even to the locals today.

The hill has a soft green slope
and is flat on the top.
Like a bathroom floor,
as smooth as can be.

When the moon is out,
and a soft wind flows,
those fairies come out
and dance and sing
until the break of day.

Soft harp music
you can also hear.
It makes you mellow
and you want to stay.

Down at the bottom
along a small stream,
is a fairy bush
oh so green.

It's a place to relax
among the trees,
and the rocks,
and have sweet dreams.

Don't touch their bush
or destroy their stones
Just love
and respect them,

for fairy hill
is their wee home.

Irish Country Road

The super highways,
the inner city with urban blight.
For me there is more in Ireland
for you to explore.

The Irish country road has more:
walk down an Irish country road,
whether in County Kerry
the gem of the south
or on the wild hills
of Tyrone in the north.
Hedges or stone walls
on either side,
small farms with all kinds of crops,
sheeps and lambs forage and play
among Ireland's green grass.

Stone bridges over trout streams,
some with one or three or even five spans.
Look over the side at the water.
It makes music as it ripples
over the rocks and the sand.

If you meet a farmer
or a stranger,
I would be surprised
if he did not say hello.

Dublin and Belfast
are cultural centers
and are exciting to see,
but give me an Irish country road,
and it is the next best thing
to heaven for me.

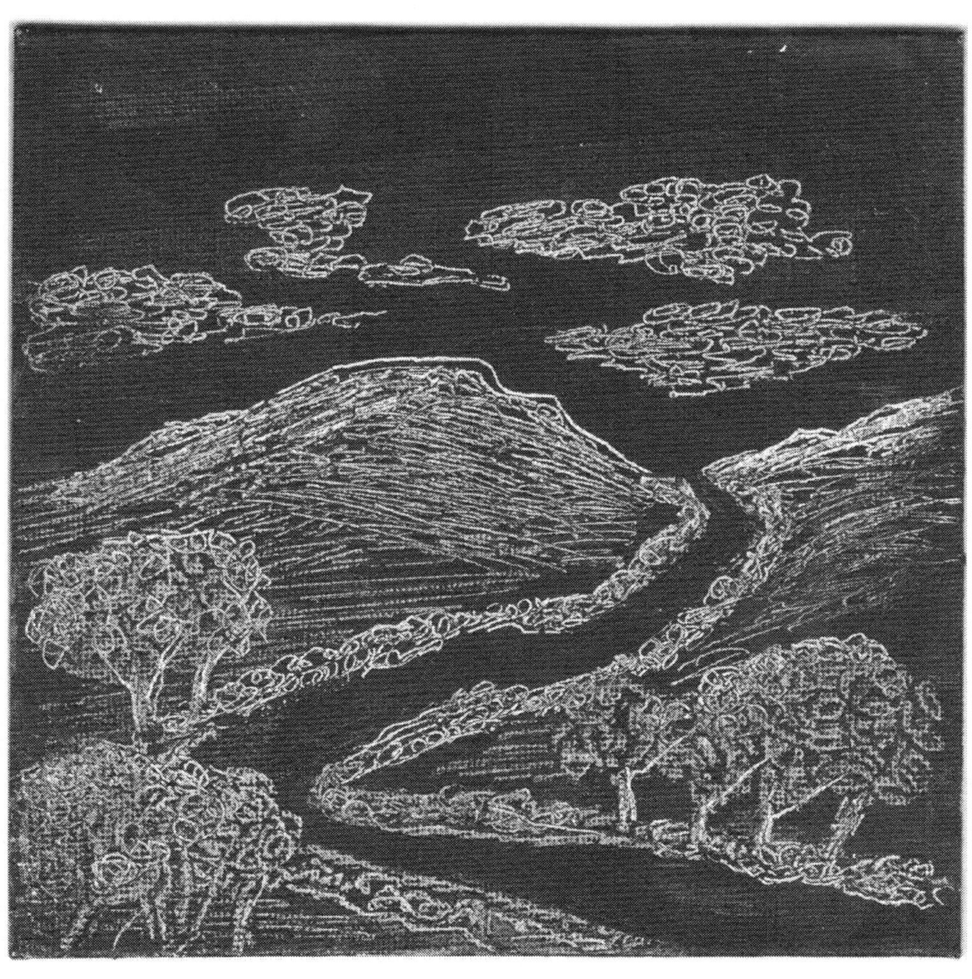

Rover the Irish Farm Dog

Rover slept in a barn
among the hay and straw.
He was black and white
with a touch of brown
on his nose
and his two front paws.

Nobody seemed to care
what kind of breed he was.
His purpose was
to work on the farm,
bring in the milk cows
and herd the sheep.
Rover's skills
on the farm
were beyond belief.

Oatmeal for breakfast
with fresh cream on top.
Now for the evening meal,
he would get scraps of beef,
and some left over
greasy Irish stew.

To clean his teeth,
he would have
the knee bone of a cow.

If he needed a bath,
he went to the stream,
and swam all about.

For bugs and fleas,
he was dipped in a tank

that was used for
lambs and sheep.

At the age of fourteen,
he passed away,
as he laid on the soft Irish meadow
straw and hay.

Being Correct: An Irish Viewpoint

Question: Is it correct to say, or to hear someone else say, the Irish drink too much?
Answer: Yes, being Irish myself, is this without a doubt, beyond correct!

Question: Is it politically correct to say, we Irish should not be ruled by the crown?
Answer: Yes, this is correct, but please do not attack the English people.

Question: For a politician to trash his opponent in a personal manner, is he or she being politically correct?
Answer: No, this is not correct, but true facts and issues are correct.

Question: Is it correct to say, Irish red-headed women have a quick temper?
Answer: It is possible this is correct, but it is a theory, not a proven fact.

Question: Is it correct to say there is no such thing as Irish gourmet?
Answer: This is correct, but if you like Irish soda bread, potatoes and stout, it is incorrect to say there is no such thing as Irish gourmet.

STOUT

The Wind

Oh, how destructive
the wind can be:
cyclones, tornados, hurricanes.
Nature's untamed force,
it can be.

But think of the good,
and where would ancient commerce be.
The wind,
did those sailing ships need.

The Vikings traveled
the north atlantic,
and to distant shores
they went.

Wind scatters seeds
from flowering plants,
and with the help
of an early frost,
removes dead leaves
from trees.

The wind moves
the blades of windmills
to pump water from aquifers
or America's thirsty plains.

You can't see the wind
as it moves through
tall pine trees.
But sweet music
it makes.
You can't tame the wind,

only one person did.

When the Lord
spoke to the wind,
it obeyed,
and it was calm.

The Headless Horseman

In the soft rolling hills of
southeast County Down,
the headless horseman rides.

This is his domain,
to this he lays claim.
Was he a commoner
in years gone by,
or someone of fame?
Could he have been beheaded
by that villain, Cromwell?
For his dress and attire
fits in with that time.
The sword that he carries
is pure white.
And at the tip
comes out a red glow.

The horse that he rides
is a black stallion
above average in height.
The reins and the bridle
shine like silver at night.
The horse seems to guide him
in the direction
he wants to go,
and the horse's eyes give off
a green glow.

Whenever he is seen,
good follows his path.
Stone hedges
on widows' farms
are repaired and fixed.

Lost sheep are
put back in their pastures,
and wooden gates
that were left open,
are closed and locked.

So don’t be afraid of
this ghostly figure,
that rides and resides
in the Mourne mountains
in southeast County Down.

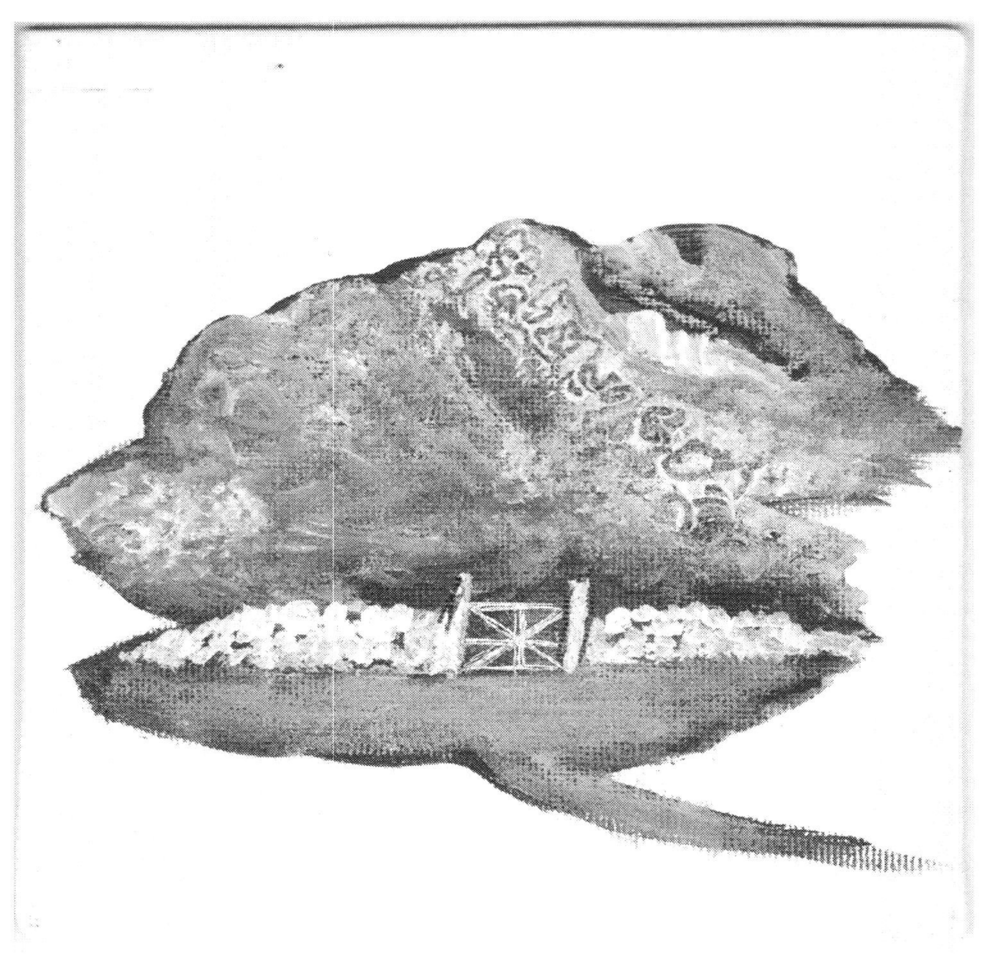

Words

Words
spoken or written
can heal or destroy.

Before you speak,
think things over:
they can't be retrieved or brought back.

Jesus spoke words
that were perfect,
when he spoke about evil and good.

His words
healed the sick,
brought calm to the sea.
Words of hope
beyond question,
he gave to us all.

He gave words
of assurance
that through him
there would be life after death.

Evil men
have spoken words
with venom and hate.
Wars come about,
people displaced,
slaughtered and killed,
because of their religion or race.

Let us speak words
that will heal,
and bring about peace.

It can happen,
if we speak words that are good.

Looking Back

Looking back on life,
I try to remember
when my journey began.

From childhood,
I was part of
God's plan.
For what reason,
I don't understand.
I have failed him,
and come up short
in so many ways.

His mercy and grace
is beyond what I deserve.
Death has tried
to conquer me
time after time,
but I am still here,
and that is only
because of him.

But tomorrow
belongs to God,
and if I see another tomorrow,
and another sunrise,
I owe it to him.

Life is not easy,
and at times,
I have wanted to give up.
Dark clouds
have gathered around me,
but his light has always

come through.

God will protect you,
don't give up!
Remember
there is life beyond,
for God does exist.

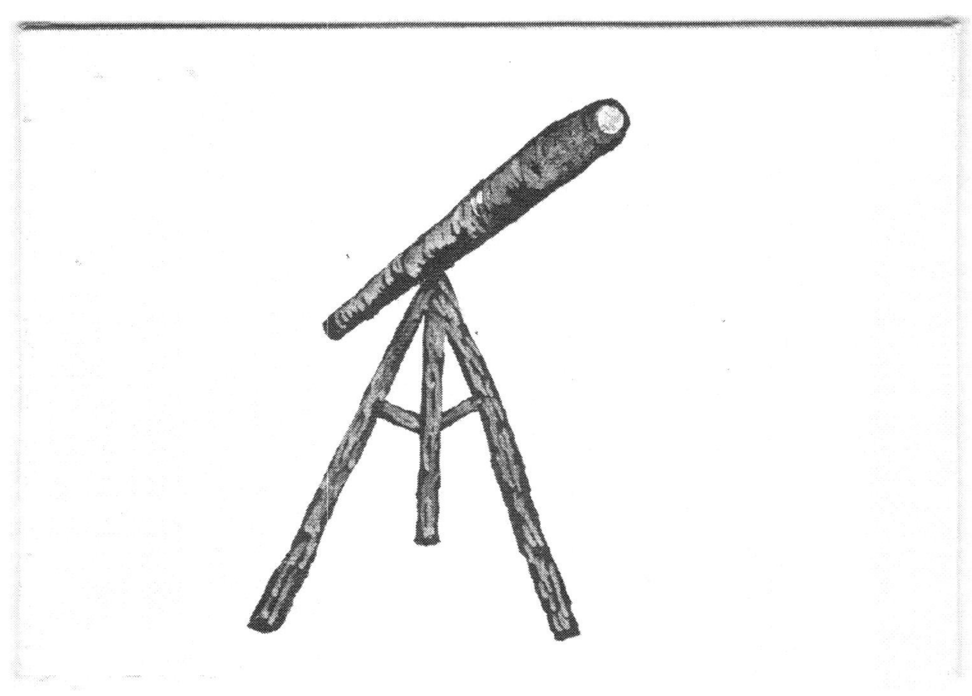

Irish Spring

Mornings full of dew and mist,
Green hills and mountain peaks
are hidden from one's view.

Warm rays of sun appear,
and you know
an Irish spring is here.
Wildflowers are abundant
everywhere.
Their beauty,
one can not compare.

The robins chirp
and sing their songs.
Sheep graze contented
on hills so green.
Knowingly into this world
new lambs they bring.

Clear mountain streams
so full of trout
makes the angler
come alert.

The farmer ploughs
soft green fields
and sows the seed,
for livestock and family
he must feed.

Soft grey clouds gather
over hills and mountain peaks.
Their soft rain
they will release.

Neighbors greet each other
with a smile.
Come in for tea
and stay awhile.
This is what an Irish spring
is all about.

Antrim Glens

Walk down those glens
with the hills
covered in heather
on every side.

The streams softly ripple
over the rocks
and the sand.

The trout swim fast
and jump over
small waterfalls.

Wildflowers
cover the banks
of the streams.
Soft yellow and purple,
their scent fills the air.

Few places in Ireland
with these glens
you can compare.
As on the glens
near the sea,
majestic waterfalls
you will want to see.
The music they make,
makes you want to
go back in time.

When the ancient Celts
came to these glens,
a little bit of heaven
they did find.

Peace and contentment
will fill your soul,
and back to the city
you won't want to go.

Evil Oliver

Oliver Cromwell
came to Ireland
in sixteen-forty-nine
with an army
of ten thousand strong.

He marched on Drogheda,
a city about thirty miles
north of Dublin.
He destroyed the city
with heavy cannons,
and put their two thousand Irish garris
onto the sword.

The fertile land
of the north and the east
was confiscated
and given to his army,
then they divided the spoil.

Cromwell had little desire
to invade western Ireland,
which included
County Galway and Mayo.
He was reported
to have said these words:
"There is not a tree to hang a man,
too rocky to bury a man,
and not enough soil to grow food
to feed a man."

Maybe he saw no beauty
in the pristine lakes,
and fast flowing streams

laden with salmon and trout.
This evil man's eyes
should have been open
to see the beauty
of Ireland's west.

Sound Memories

The sound of a waterfall
in a hidden glen
as it cascades over
rocks and plunges
to depths below.

The sound of rain
on a tin roof
while inside
an old stone barn.

The sound of a rooster
on a nearby farm
as it tells you
it is time to get up.

The sound of crickets
on the hearth,
beside a black peat open fire.

And the perking of
an old black kettle,
saying I'm ready to make
you some tea.

The sound of bagpipes
coming down the glen
it's given you warmth
beyond anything else,
and a protective feeling as well.

The sound of frogs
in a peat bog,
it's different

but enjoyable to hear.

The sound of sheep and lambs
on an Irish spring morning
as they forage
on Ireland's green grass.

The sound of my mother's voice
so reassuring.
Kindness and love
you heard in her voice.

Leprechaun Encounter

I met a little leprechaun
while working down the glen.
He had a large silver buckle on his hat
that glittered and sparkled
as he moved his head.

When he spoke
it was with a strange Irish accent,
neither north or south.
His long beard to his waist
it did go,
and was as white as
pure mountain snow.

His eyes
they did twinkle
and gave off a strange glow.
He gave me a small buckle,
and a lace from his shoe.
Then he said with a giggle,
O, sir, how do you do?
Make a wish for yourself
and it will come true.

But before I could answer,
he corrected himself.
The pot of gold at the end of the rainbow
is for me not you!

In the flash of a second
he then disappeared
Where he vanished to,
I don't really know.

He was a cute little fellow
about twelve inches tall.
The only wish that I want
is for him to come back
and say well hello.

Irish Stew

Growing up in Ireland I had my fill of Irish stew. It was a poor man's meal made from mutton, not lamb. There is a difference - believe me. My personal view of Irish stew would keep me off the Irish tourism board - that's for sure.

Cut up some mutton
bite size of course
add in carrots, onions, potatoes
and that more than a few.
Boil until the mutton is well cooked,
carrots, potatoes and all.
The fat from the mutton will rise to the top
when you let it cool.
Scoop off as much fat as you can.
This is mutton,
not Irish spring lamb.
Then heat it up again
until it is nice and hot.
Service with hot Irish soda bread,
and that is that.
If some of us Irish call this gourmet,
I'll go out to the barn
and feast on some hay.

MUTTON
POTATOES
CARROTS
ONIONS

City Birds

They live in the city with we humans.
All around, everywhere, they can be found.
How they could be happy is beyond me.
When there is wide open spaces
as far as you can see.

There are mountains,
green forests with all kinds of trees.
Berries and nuts in the forest,
fish in the lakes and streams.

Drive into the parking lot of
one of these fast food chains,
and what do you see?
All kinds of birds eating the crumbs of fast food.

Greasy french fries
and crumbs from hamburger buns,
with almost zero whole grains.
You won't find a lean pigeon among the whole lot.

Hand outs from humans
white bread and table scraps.
Go to the city parks,

and the ducks and geese eat that.
But I'm afraid most of the city birds are with us to stay.
If we feed them,
let it be seed or whole grains.

CITY
BIRDS

Trust Me

Beware when a politician says these words:
trust me.
Some say it with a smirk or a grin,
and you can't discern by their looks
how they think.

They will bash their opponent,
accusing him or her of lies.
Don't they know
their own lying is a sin?

They strut when they walk,
move their hands when they talk.
It's called body language,
it's done to impress,
and with some people,
it is a success.

We will tax the rich,
and give the excess to the poor.
If they would tax their own riches,
it would put a dent in the national debt.

Beware when you see their grin,
and their smirk on national TV.
You could hear these words,
so loud, so clear:
trust me.

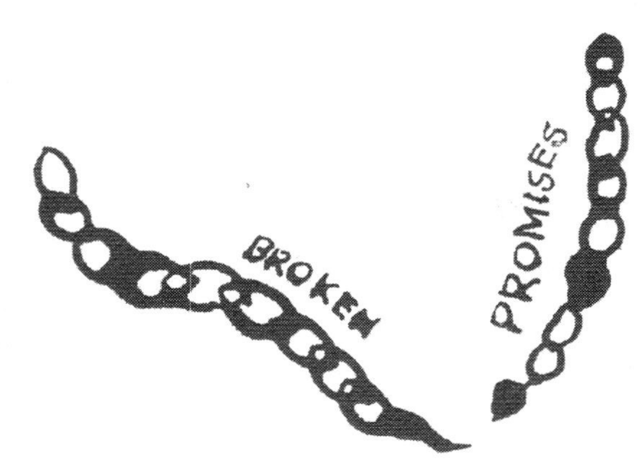
BROKEN
PROMISES

Prayer

The place for prayer can be anywhere:
a secluded place
a mountain peak
or in the valley deep below.

God hears your voice,
and knows the quiet thoughts
within your soul.
God's ear is always open
to listen to your needs,
and his eyes are never closed.

Prayer is more important than
all the arsenal of the world.
It wins more wars and battles
than the sword has ever done.

A mighty healing power
is always there,
and that power is prayer.

The world is full of hunger
and filled with war and strife.
Pray for those that hunger,
and for all to live in peace.

Families are divided,
separated and divorced.
A modern society filled with problems
that only God can solve.

Irish Winters

Underneath the snow
there are still many shades of green.
The sheep forage among the hills,
their heavy coat will keep them warm
until the spring.

The oak, ash and weeping willow trees
sparkle like crystal clothed with ice,
so clear, so bright.

Robins still come
and sit on cottage window sills,
looking for grain
or crumbs of whole wheat bread.

Hot tea or coffee,
oatmeal with cream
beside an open fire.
What else would one desire?

Children skate
and slide on shallow ponds,
for rarely does the ice get thick.

Farmers work
inside their homes,
repairing equipment
that is needed to farm.

The fox still comes out
of his cosy wee den.
Beware he could steal
the farmer's hens.

Winters in Ireland
are not dull,
people sing and play.
Maybe a sip of Irish whiskey
once or twice a day.

Do Not Enter

Don't enter into
Irish political debates,
Only when you are calm
and respect other views,
otherwise emotion takes over
and logic is out.
That's why the country is divided
for almost one hundred years.

Don't enter into
business with family,
it seldom works.
In-laws become outlaws
in a very short time.

Husbands don't enter into
an argument with their wives.
Don't be condescending,
her side of the argument
could be right.

Don't enter into
shady business deals,
money and wealth that come
by this way
are morally wrong.

Don't enter into
a forest
not knowing
the direction you're in.
Look for the moss
on the north side of a tree,
then you know what is

south, west and east.

Because He Lives

Because he lives,
I can face every problem
of tomorrow.

The moral fiber
of God's word
will keep you
safe and strong.

He is alive and well
and within our hearts
just let him dwell.

God's word is
full of truth
don't spin or
distort the facts.

He spoke about
the end of time:
earthquakes
and much more.

Please believe me,
what he said isn't folklore.
We are not alone
because of him,
that assurance is
in God's word.

So when things go wrong,
and you feel
you can't go on,
look up

his hand is there,
and he will bring you
out of all despair.

The Little Cloud

The little cloud
came over the mountain
as happy as could be.
He looked all around
and what a disappointment that he found.
The trees and the grass were turning all yellow and brown.
He said to himself
an alarm must be sent.,
so back over the mountain he went.
He gathered his friends and they formed huge clouds.
So thick, so grey, but in full array,
together we must do what is right,
and release all our rain.
Don't worry
we can get together and form again.
Now out of the heavens,
the thunder did roar,
and the lightning flashed.
The birds began to sing,
and the bees did buzz,
and to the flowers for nectar they went.
The farmer looked up with joy on his face,
and thanked God for his mercy and grace.

The Perfect Meal

If the Irish potato is grown in sandy soil,
the flavor is better by far.
If the skin cracks open when boiled,
it's perfect.

The stout should be poured
with a bartending skill,
too often it's not.

Soda bread off the griddle,
or made in a cast iron pot.
Country butter direct from the farm,
a little salt, black pepper,
and you are ready to eat.

You cut the potato open,
put country butter down the middle,
and up the sides.
Butter some hot Irish soda bread, too.

You sip on a cold stout,
as the gourmet food goes down,
say to the world:
We Irish know what gourmet food is all about!

POTATO
STOUT
SODA BREAD

Don't Compare

Don't compare
your wife's skills
with someone you know
in your own workplace.

Even if your wife's skills
are better or worse,
don't compare your wife's cooking
to your mother's
with these words,
"this is the way
mother cooked a certain meal."
That is a no.
This is a don't
many times over.

Never say
another lady's hair is beautiful.
You could get a glare,
and maybe a few words.
Besides,
you don't want to hurt her feelings.

Don't compare
your wife's make up
with other women.
That won't work.
Let her decide
how she looks
not you.

If your wife has sisters,
don't compare her looks or traits
with them,

let her be number one,
no comparisons,
please.

My Father's House

My father's house
was built with fieldstone,
whitewashed with limestone,
and thatched with wheat straw.

Hard red clay
covered the cottage floor.
A hemp mat outside
the rustic wooden door.

The children slept
on a loft above,
and the warm peat fire
kept them cozy in the wintertime.
In the open fireplace,
burned black peat.
The sweet aroma
would make you stay
and not retreat.

A large cast iron pot
cooked the food,
potatoes, oatmeal, or Irish stew.
In the dark black kettle,
strong Irish black tea
did brew.

A natural spring
gave water to the household
located outside the garden wall.
It was a source of plenty
in the winter, spring, summer and fall.

The small garden

grew potatoes, apples, turnips,
and so much more.

At my father's house,
a stranger was always welcomed
when he stepped through
this Irish cottage door.

Freedom

The eagle soars
to the heavens above,
its massive wings outstretched.
It has the freedom
it deserves
to soar,
rising above the sea,
and highest mountain peaks.

A wide world of freedom
to the eagle is everywhere,
for those piercing eagle eyes to see.

Salmon
have the freedom
to go up rivers
through rapids and churning foam,
and there to spawn.

The tortoise
has the freedom
to crawl at its own pace,
and hide within its shell
when humans do intrude.

The common field mouse
has the freedom
to eat some grain
from the golden wheat fields
on the plains.

God give us all the freedom to
worship, dance, and play,
and we will thank you everyday.

Life Beyond

There will be no graveyards
on the hillsides of heaven,
no death or funerals to attend,
no need for the sun or the moon
to shine their light.
For we will walk in
the light of our Lord.

No hunger or thirst
will be in heaven,
for our heavenly bodies
won't require earthly needs.

Jesus said
in the world to come,
there would be many mansions.
But I would be contented
with what looks like
a cozy Irish cottage
if God allows me
to be up there.

The High King Brian Boru

Brian Boru,
you were the high king
of all Ireland,
and with an army
of better warriors,
you defeated the vikings,
and drove them out.

The final battle was
at Clontarf
in the year ten fourteen.
You did not stay
behind the battle lines,
and order your men to fight.
But into the heat of battle
with your warriors
you went.

You had no fear,
king Brian Boru.
We Irish are
so proud of you.
You were tall
and had massive arms
and shoulders,
with your body' strength,
you were endowed to fight.
Your sword so huge,
and you could wield it
with one arm or both.

You gave up your life
On Clontarf battlefield
a hero,

no one doubts.
The mighty Vikings
were defeated one for all,
history does recall.

Your tomb is in
the ancient city of Armagh,
the place they say Saint Patrick
built his first church.
We Irish honor you high king,
the awesome warrior Brian Boru.

Never Fades

God's love is always bright
and never fades.
With God there is perfect order
of all that's right.

Roses form and bud
and blossom forth,
and slowly fade away.
Allow God's love to be
in your heart,
it, too, will blossom
but never fade away.
It will forever stay.

Spring comes
after winter's snow and ice
Buds appear
and the leaves turn green.
But then again,
when fall sets in
those leaves fade
and fall
and turn to dust.

Time does not cause
God's promises to fade
for they are eternal
in what he said.

The Miser

John Magee was going on eighty five years old - his body was tired, just worn out, from doing hard manual work for most of his life. His only son, Sean, lived about three miles away, and Sean would drop in to see his father at least a few times a week. He never got upset with his father's strange ways; as they would say in Ireland, "he is just not right."

Sean's wife, Jean, would send a basket of food at least once a week to give to Sean's father. John Magee would not spend one penny for food unless he had to. For the most part, he was a recluse, and kept to himself. John would sit by the fireplace from morning to night, and he would do stone carvings, which his son sold to gift shops, and gave his father the money. For sixty years, John worked at a stone quarry and received a paycheck every week. John would say to his son, "I have a secret place to keep my pound notes for I don't trust banks." Not a penny John would spend on his own unless he had to - he was a miser of the worst kind.

Winter arrived early, and there was ice and snow on the ground. John thought a deep freeze was coming, so he went to the well to stock up on fresh water, and he had two large buckets with him. The rough stone path to the well was covered with ice. It caused John to fall with his head first on the ice. It must have been around five in the afternoon before it got dark. The following morning, his son Sean came by, but could not find his father in the house. Going outside, he found his father lying still on the ground. He had died from the fall, and his body was frozen and stiff. Sean rushed back to his house and brought Jean back with him, so they could carry the body back inside. Sean gave his father a respectful funeral, and they would have a headstone placed at the gravesite at a later date. About two weeks later, Sean and Jean with their two sons decided to go through the house and clean it out.

Sitting at the table having some tea, Jean asked the question, "What do you think? Your father did not believe in banks. What did he do with all that money?" Sean replied, "Yes, you are right. He often said that, and he even once said to me that there would be a surprise in the house after he was gone." "So very strange," Jean replied.

Sean and Jean began to clean again, and they decided to move the bed to the center of the bedroom so that they could wash the floors underneath. As they were moving the bed, Sean and Jean noticed a large hemp matt. Once the two lifted up the matt, they discovered a carved door built into the wooden floor. "But what for?," Jean uttered, astonished.

Placing two fingers through the small latch, Sean pulled the door open - a musty smell filled the air with a small cloud of dust. Sean and Jean gazed at each other for a moment, then John naturally said, "let's see what's inside." The dust had cleared somewhat, and they came upon two boxes made out of wood. One was much larger than the other. They took out the smaller one first, and when they opened it up, it contained Sean's mother's wedding ring in addition to her watch and all different kinds of trinkets and coins. Reaching further down inside, Sean proceeded to remove the larger box. As Sean was removing the box from the vault, he heard a cracking noise, and the box quickly fell apart.

Dust once again filled the air, and when the dust had settled, Jean and Sean received a surprise - in the box, his father had stacked hundreds of pound notes, but they were in small fragments, combined with dust and dirt. Rats and mice had chewed holes in the box, destroying the pound notes. Sixty years worth of savings went down the tubes. Yes, John the miser should have put his pound notes in a steel box or in the bank. If John had made a will out, maybe it would have read like this: I leave all my wealth to the mice and rats!

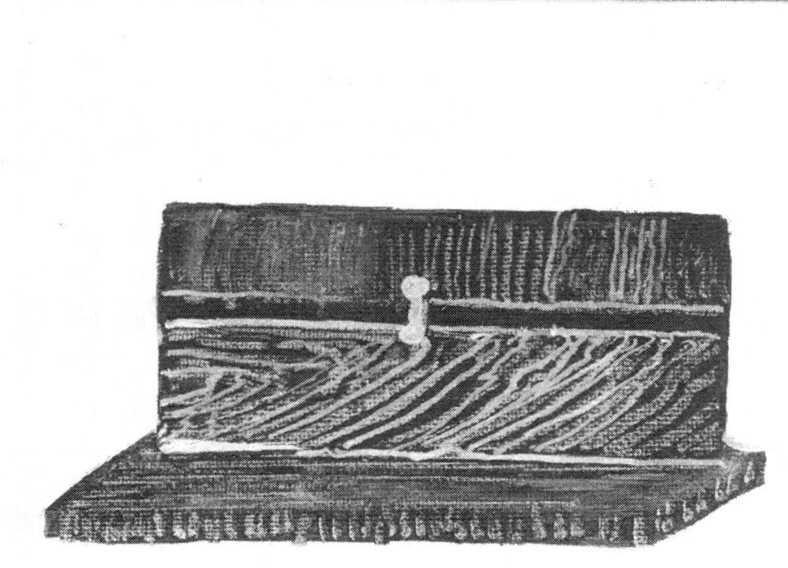

Irish Potheen

Potheen is illicitly distilled whiskey made for home consumption, and sometimes for sale. County Leitrim in northwest Ireland is famous for this whiskey. They make the number one claim to it. The fine mist in those hills and glens hide the smoke from their stills. They call it white lightning in the Kentucky hills. It's made out of corn, barley or rye. In Ireland, potatoes are used to make this illicit drink. Maybe it is one hundred proof - do you think? Some say that this whiskey is medicinal - good for one's health. I can't agree with this excuse for drinking. Don't go to County Leitrim, and ask to buy this whiskey. The locals there don't trust strangers, and their neighbors, just a few.

POTEEN

Body Language

Not a word needs to be spoken:
through body language,
a message can be sent.
Some politicians would never be elected,
if observation was our first choice.
There are good honest men in all parties
and women as well,
and they don't use body language to impress.

President Lincoln had a profile
of courage and honesty,
and it showed all over his face.

General Lee,
a renowned confederate general,.
when he sat tall and upright in his saddle,
he gave incentive to his army to fight.

General Patton,
an American hero, no doubt.
The look in his eyes,
and the stern look on his face,
It put fear in the enemy before a cannon was fired.

Now give a wave to a neighbor,
put a smile on your face.
You have made an impression without a word being said.
Shake the hands of a stranger,
with soft eye contact,
and a smile when you look in his face.

It's a mirror to him or her
what you are
even before a word has been said.

This is body language at its best.

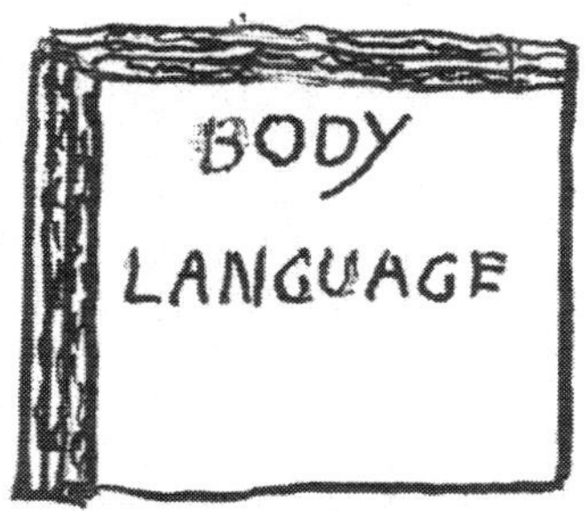

Cholesterol Plus

Old fashioned Irish fish and chips
were not healthy,
but they sure tasted good.
Hot lard oil is what they were cooked in -
both the fish and the chips.
White flour and eggs,
and a pinch of baking soda
were used to make the batter for the fish.
The lard gave the fish a unique flavor
not found in modern day fish and chips.
Old newspapers were wrapped
into the shape of a cone,
and into the cone,
the fish and chips went.
The hot grease from the lard
would come through the paper,
and it did not take long for that to happen.
Because of the cholesterol,
regardless of taste,
modern day fish and chips
are healthier to eat.

LARD
FLOUR

Vanished

The Irish linen trade is almost gone.
Factory chimneys no longer belch out gray smoke.
That smoke you could have seen from miles away.
Now the sky is clear
and you can breath the air,
so fresh.

Lurgan, Lisburn and Belfast
were the linen centers of the north.
Your factories are silent,
tall chimneys torn down.
You are a sad memory of the past.

Work was hard, wages low.
The linen barons were the upper class,
and wealthy mansions they did own.
Row houses were provided
for some of the working class,
crowded into narrow streets.

Catholics lived in one area of town,
separated from the Protestants
that had mostly Scottish names.

Protestants were given the choice of jobs,
and ads in the local papers
would say only Protestants need apply.
It was discrimination at its worst.

Competition from overseas,
cotton,
cheap labor elsewhere
caused the Irish linen trade to disappear.

Irish linen was the best,
it was the cloth of kings and queens,
and it was known throughout the world for its quality.
Unemployment is high in the old Irish linen towns.
Some new industry has come in,
but not enough to sustain the population's growth.

The Well Digger

John Haney was a well digger, and one of the best in town. But he was known to sip on Irish Whiskey from morning to night. He used a pick and a shovel until he reached hard rock. Then with a small amount of explosives, John would blast the rock. He used a winch to haul debris to the top, and also to lower the digger down into the well and bring him back up. The rope had to be checked at times to see if it was frayed or worn out, because the grit and the gravel could slowly etch away at the rope and make it weak. Down the well John would go shovel with explosives and all. He always had a bottle of whiskey tucked into his warm shirt.

Outside the village of Moira, a well had to be dug, and John Haney was hired to dig a deep well. The well reached the depth of thirty feet, and a small amount of explosives was needed to loosen the rock beforehand.

Early one Monday morning, John was lowered down into the well - He had already chiseled out a hole,he now packed in the explosives and lit the fuse. John had ten minutes to get out of the well, and he needed to be hoisted to the top. But, the rope suddenly frayed and broke. John was stuck.

Luckily, though, there were at least six locals at the top of the well, and they threw a spare rope down and told John to tie it under his arms or around his waist, and to do it fast. John yelled back, "I will drink my whiskey first and leave the bottle down here. If the Whiskey's inside of me, it won't be destroyed in the blast." The locals yelled from the top, "let us get you out of the well now, you whiskey drinking fool!" John replied with a laugh, "I still have time to sip the last drop. I've got at least another three minutes, maybe more."

John sipped down the last drop, and yelled, "get me out of here or this will be the last sip of my life." The locals pulled him up just in time with about thirty seconds to spare. Then John remarked, "If I would've died in the blast, do you think the devil has good Irish whiskey down there?"

Being Sacked

This is based on a true story, and the story includes most of the facts.

In Ireland, if you were sacked, it meant you had lost your job. The country roads in Ireland always needed repair - potholes and cracks, and with so much rain, it caused the foundations of some roads to erode. Workers would put down hot coal tar, then apply the crushed rock on top.

A prosperous small businessman called Charlie Spencer owned a hard rock quarry in Moira, which is in County Down. He had a few lorries, which in America, they call trucks. Charlie also had a few steam rollers to flatten the crushed rock on top of the coal tar to make a smooth surface, and most of the time, it worked.

Mr. Spencer was a soft spoken man, and generous; he was very good to his help. But he was strict about drinking, and for drinking on the job, you would be sacked. John McClurg, one of the lorry drivers, liked to take a few drinks during working hours. He would hide his lorry under bushes and trees in a grove not far from one of the local pubs. Then John would go into the pub through the back door so that he would not be seen.

Well, one day Mrs. Spencer was going by the pub on the way to do some shopping in a nearby town. Glancing over, she noticed a lorry somewhat hidden in a grove of trees next to the pub. She got out of her car to further investigate, and found out it was one of the quarry's lorries. She hid in some bushes for about ten minutes to see if someone would come out of the pub. Then she noticed John through some trees trying to stay out of sight. She did not approach John, since her husband owned the quarry and he would take care of the problem.

Over the course of a few days, Mr. Spencerr pondered what to do since he liked John in a personal way, but he couldn't tolerate drinking on the job. Friday evening around 5 pm, John pulled in with his lorry, and Mr. Spencer was waiting and had a stern look on his face. John parked his lorry and went to the quarry office to get his pay for the week. Mr. Spencer was there, gave John his pay for the week, and then bluntly said, "you're sacked, and I don't want to see you within ten miles of my quarry again! I've had it with you, Mr. McClurg. You've been drinking during working hours, and don't deny what I am saying to you is not true. As of this moment, you are sacked! Do you have anything to say? I would like to hear your response." Mr. McClurg humbly replied, "I don't blame you, Mr. Spencer. You are doing the right thing by sacking me. I've had it coming for a long time now."

John got on his bike and waved goodbye to Mr. Spencer, and home to his family, he went. He gave his wife his paycheck but never mentioned a word about being sacked. Monday morning, his wife woke him up and said, "John, you need to hurry; Mr. Spencer frowns on latecomers to work." John ate some Irish oatmeal, and with it, two cups of black Irish tea. Then he got on his bike, and rode to the quarry. Coming through the gate, Mr. Spencer met John. "Why are you here, Mr. McClurg?," shouted Mr. Spencer, "You have been sacked as of this past Friday." Mr McClurg boldly replied, "Yes, that's true. You did sack me on Friday, and I'm hoping you won't do it again today. So let me on by, and I'll start my lorry up." Mr. Spencer gasped in shock, and said these words, "I give up!" In the end, Mr. McClurg was sacked for two whole days, and his wife never found out about what happened. John stopped his drinking and Mr. Spencer made him foreman over the whole quarry because with other men, he had a personal touch.

SACKED

The Grave Digger

The grave digger in Ireland was a part time occupation that people held in respect. In the vault of the church all the maps of the gravesites were kept. In South Antrim about twenty two miles southwest of Belfast was a small village called Soldiernstown. The village was named after Oliver Cromwell's army. His army camped there on his march north, and many of the old churches he used heavy cannon on them and the destruction is everywhere to be found. Soldierstown graveyard is not as old as many of the others in that area. I would say about two hundred and fifty years old. The gravedigger was a small man by the name of Harry Adams, eccentric so the locals did say. But he got into trouble when he visited the McDowell farm. Mr. McDowell had been sick for a very long time, but he was slowly recovering, and his wife was happy about that. Harry Adams came by to visit the McDowell's, but his motive was clear. He was not as concerned about Mr. McDowell's health as much as the fee he would get for opening up the grave when and if Mr. McDowell passed away. The McDowells had four burial plots at the Soldierstown graveyard and many of his family had been buried there before. More than one person could be buried in the same single plot. The law was after seven years, another coffin or casket could be placed on top since embalming was seldom done, and it did not take long for the coffin to rot, and the body return to dust.

Sitting beside Mr. McDowell's bed, Harny did not ask "were you getting better?" or "how do you feel?" He was thinking about the fee he would get for digging the grave. Out of Harry's mouth came these words: "you are going to die, so what plot do you want to be in? Your father's? Or your mother's? You need to decide because I need to start getting things ready." Mrs. McDowell was washing pots and pans in the kitchen, and came with a small frying pan in her hand. "Get out of this house now! Or I will whack you on your bald head! You are worse than the scum that comes in with the tide!" Harry ran out of the house with his hands covering his bald head. Mrs. McDowell yelled out, "You will never get a fee for opening up a McDowell grave. When you die, make sure your money is in your coffin. Maybe you can buy a ticket to the place far below that is where you are going to go!

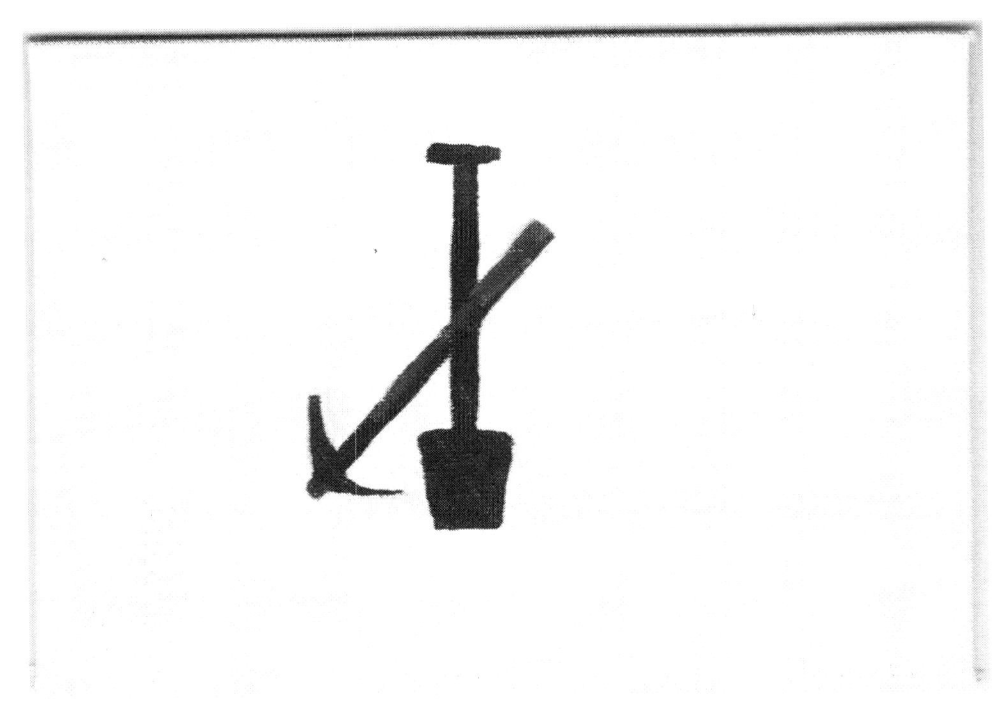

Best Friends - Maybe

Tyrone and Mindy lived at the home of the O'Rileys. Tyrone the dog was called after the county in which Brian his son resided. Mindy was the name Mrs. O'Riley wanted to call the cat. The O'Riley's home was about six miles north of the city of Cork. Mr. O'Riley, a bricklayer, built the house out of red bricks. It was more of a burnt orange than red, but the locals called it red. The blue gray slate imported from Wales was called "Bangor blue." With the cottage, there was a half acre of land, where the O'Rileys had a huge garden full of turnips, carrots, cabbage, and of course Irish potatoes. They had a son named Brian who lived in county Tyrone about forty miles west of Belfast. Brian was the manager of a large grocery store. He and his wife Kathleen and their three sons would visit the folks down in Cork about six times a year. Being just the two of them, they decided to get a dog, which Mr. O'Riley wanted, but Mrs. O'Riley wanted a Russian blue cat, a pedigree, no doubt.

Robert her husband was not happy at all. Paying money for a cat did not sit well with him. But Brenda, his wife, got her way. There was a breeder in the city that bred top of the line Russian blues, and that's what Brenda wanted, nothing else. All Mrs. O'Riley could say when she brought the female kitten home, "how cute! It's adorable!" It about drove Robert crazy. "I like the name Mindy," Brenda said, "it gives the cat a sense of royality, and she is a pedigree after all." After Mindy got used to her new home, Robert decided to get a dog that would be his, for Mindy wanted nothing to do with him. The farmer who lived about a mile away had a part border collie mixed with some other breed, and it was going to have a litter of pups. Being good friends as they were, he could pick out a male of his choice. After four months, Robert brought the puppy home, and introduced him to Mindy. Mindy looked at the cute little dog and would hiss and up on Mrs. O'Riley's lap she went, as much as to say, "what's that?" It was a relationship of low tolerance - they ignored each other for the most part. Mindy would curl on Brenda's lap, purr, kneed her stomach, and acted like the Queen of Sheba. She would play with the wool while Brenda was knitting socks, which she seldom got scoulded for. A year went by, and they were both getting more mature. It was a cold, damp early winter night, the warm fire in the fireplace was turning to embers, but the room would still be warm for a while. Robert had dozed off in the armchair, Brenda had gone to bed early as the next day she was going to take a train to Dublin to do some Christmas shopping. Mindy and Tyrone were still awake and were glaring at each other. Tyrone in his dog language said to Mindy, "we need to talk." Mindy replied, "why should I talk to a dog who's beneath me? I'm a pedigree, and I'm going to be in shows all over Ireland, and Mrs. O'Riley thinks I'll win every contest." Tyrone went on to say, after pompous Mindy stopped jabbering, "Well, at least I can guard my master's cottage, and I will defend my master against anyone that tries to harm him." "Well," said Mindy, "I can catch mice from the nearby farm, but I won't eat them - I have more dignity than that! I get fed special food since I'm a royal cat - it's not like I'm some old alley cat." "Well, let's see what else I can do, you snob," Tyrone barked out. "I can herd sheep on the nearby farm, and for a reward, I usually get a nice bone to chew on." Mindy replied, "Since I'll be winning so many contests, Mrs. O'Riley will have extra money to spend. In fact, there's a contest coming up in Dublin, and the first prize is 2,000 euros. This puts extra money into the household, so you're useless, Tyrone, compared to me!" Tyrone started to become very irritated, "Well, I can fetch balls, roll over, and play dead." Mindy promptly replied, "Well, I've got agility. Because I'm a cat, I can do better than that - I can climb trees. If you tried that, you wouldn't get to the first limb." Tyrone fiercely answered back, "you'll ruin the bark on the apple trees with your claws. I overheard a conversation earlier on - Mr. O'Riley wants to get rid of you, but since you're Mrs. O'Riley's spoiled cat, we're forced to tolerate you." The two pets went back and forth until they were tired, and finally fell asleep. Tyrone had enough of the "snob," and Mindy had enough of what she called a "useless dog."

About a month later, the O'Rileys went up north to see their son for about three days. They left warm blankets and plenty of food and water for Mindy and Tyrone. There was also a dog door in the kitchen, where they could go outside if need be.

Mindy decided to go outside and look around. It was cold but her fur kept her warm. Climbing up one of the apple trees, she started looking around the neighborhood, and then Mindy became startled. A huge Irish wolfhound was coming down the road, and it was heading towards the O'Riley's cottage. He then caught sight of Mindy up in the tree. Mindy cried out,

"Tyrone, please help me!! If I come down, the wolfhound will have me for dinner."

Tyrone heard her cry and had a change of heart. After all, Mindy is family and family comes first. Tyrone knew he couldn't take the wolfhound out by going for his head. Surprise is the key in any fight. With great speed, Tyrone ran and grabbed the back leg of the wolfhound. Tyrone had taken him off guard. Letting out a yelp, he turned and ran after Tyrone, and raged to himself, "I'll have that little dog for lunch." Tyrone ran through the kitchen doggie door, and luckily the wolfhound could only get halfway through. While this fiasco was unfolding, little scared Mindy came down from the tree, and ran behind old bricks that were stacked near the fence. The wolfhound came back into the yard, and tried to catch Mindy with one of his paws. Mindy put her claws all the way out, and scratched up the wolfhound's paw. The wolfhound had enough, and ran out of the O'Riley's yard. Seeing that everything was clear, Mindy dashed into the house, and thanked Tyrone profusely. Tyrone and Mindy became best friends, and they sat together around the fireplace. When the O'Rileys went to bed every night, they would cozy up and starting chatting.

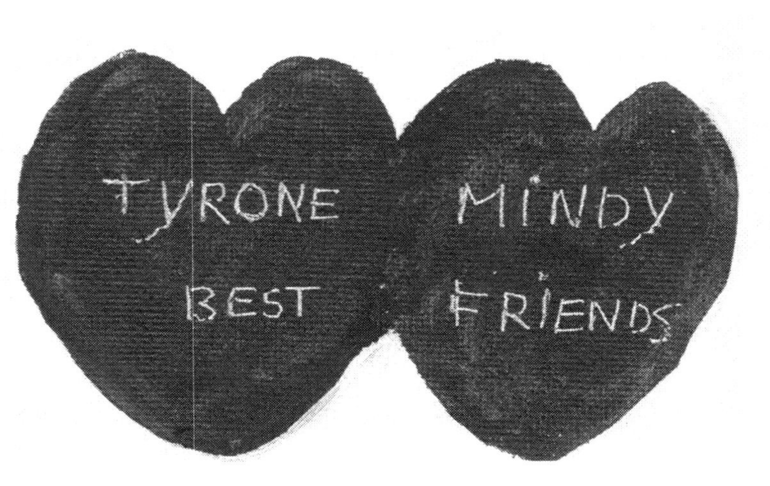
TYRONE
BEST
MINDY
FRIENDS

The Last Letter

You have denied our rights,
you evil English lords.
You lust and crave authority
more than the fine French wine
that you do drink.

The potato harvest has failed,
so little we have to eat.
But in your wheat and barley fields,
there is grain.
Not one morsel
you want to give to us,
a proud celtic race.

Don't you have a conscience?
Are you not ashamed?

The salmon in the rivers
that run through your estates,
we are not allowed to catch!
They don't belong to you.
Again, I say:
you are evil English lords.

My wife and our newborn child are buried
in the graveyard
in a wooden coffin
I made myself.
Nothing else
I could afford.

You have threatened to burn my cottage
to the ground,
your penal system is corrupt.
Tomorrow you can do

what your evil mind decides to do,
for I will be gone.

Even now in my mind,
I see the port of Derry
so bright, so clear.
I, John Murphy,
will board what they call a coffin ship.
I will have a fee to pay
But I have to leave
my wife and newborn child,
so, so, so sad I feel inside.

To America,
with God's help,
I will arrive
and breath the freedom
we Irish all deserve.

I'm not angry
with the English working man,
and the few lords
that are kind,
and share our plight.
They are good people,
and they know what is right.

On my way to Derry,
I will stop by the graveyard,
and to you,
Kathleen,
and our son,
I will say a last goodbye.

KATHLEN
MURPHY
1825 - 1845
SON
SEAN
1845

The Texan

Billy Randall, a young Texan, had just graduated from a Texas university with high honors. One of his degrees was in business, and the other related to farming and ranching. His father owned a huge ranch near Kerrsville in the Texas hill country. Great ranching country, if not the best in Texas. Billy was handsome, about 6'2" in height with blue eyes and reddish brown hair. His hobby was rodeo, and even at an early age in his life, he was very successful, and had won first place many times. Billy was well known on the rodeo circuit nationwide. He was very arrogant at times, and he thought he knew twice as much as his father, and five times more than his grandfather. At times, he and his father would butt heads like big horned sheep, and even lock horns.

One day at an early Texas breakfast consisting of steak and eggs, and of course grits with Texas-sized slices of toast, Billy started the conversation off by saying, "I want to go back to Ireland, and trace my ancestral roots." "This is a good idea," his father replied. Curtis, his father, went on to say, "We are what they call "Scotch Irish" from Ulster, the northern province of Ireland. There is a small town in Country Antrim called 'Randallstown,' and that's where the Randalls came during the plantation of Ulster. We came to Ulster from Scotland in the 1600s. The Scotch-Irish were not given the same rights as others in Ulster, including no freedom from the crown as well as religious freedom. Thousands left Ulster and settled in Virginia and the Carolinas. Here we are in Texas, the proud descendents of the Scotch-Irish. Now, Billy, I have something to say to you: don't go over to Ireland with a know-it-all attitude, which you have." Billy responded, "I know a lot, dad, and I'm going to Ireland to teach those Irish farmers how to ranch and farm Texas-style."

It was early spring, and Billy hopped on a plane to Dublin, and then a train to Belfast, almost 90 miles to the north. Getting off the train, Billy inquired, "How do I get to Randallstown? Will you please tell me?" The young lady at the ticket office gave Billy a smile, and of course, she noticed how handsome he was. "Well, you can take a bus that goes out there once a day, or rent a car." Smiling again, she proceeded to say, "Make sure you drive on the left side of the road. As I know by your accent, you're American." Billy tipped his hat, and said, "I'm not only from America! I'm from the great state of Texas." There was a slightly arrogant tone in his voice. "May I introduce myself? I'm Sandra Blair. I attend Queens University, and I work part time here at the train station." "Thank you, Sandra, for your help," and then Billy started walking away. Suddenly, Billy spun around on the heels of his handmade cowboy boots, and said, "Sorry Sandra for being so rude. I forgot to introduce myself: I'm Billy Randall from Kersville, Texas." Sandra says, "Thank you for coming back. I was about to call after you, and tell you I'd be willing to drive you to Randallsville tomorrow, since it's my day off." "Would you do that? I would enjoy the company of an attractive young lady like you. You're as pretty and sweet as Texas young sage." Billy replied. "Turn off your Texan charm for now," Sandra replied. "I've got to get to know you first, and then you can turn it back on." Billy stayed at a small hotel close to the train station, and had a good night's sleep.

Sandra picked Billy up around 8 am, and gave Billy a warm smile, and said, "We're going to have a wonderful day." "That we are! Thank you for everything, Sandra," Billy said. They arrived in Randallstown about 45 minutes later. It was a clear, crisp spring morning. A little mist on the edge of the hills overlooking the fertile river valley of the upper river Bann. "Let us go to the cemetery first, Billy, and look at the headstones. I'm sure there are some Randalls buried there." Sandra went on to say, "I was thinking of you all night long, and some of my thoughts were about finding your ancestors. Don't think it morbid of me that I thought the cemetery would be a good place to start." "Yes, I came prepared also. I bought a flat pudding knife and a soft wire brush, so if we have to remove moss off from the headstones, we can." On the outskirts of town, Sandra and Billy came across an old cemetery. The church was in ruins, but the gravesites were especially well kept up. They both searched for about ten minutes, and then Sandra yelled out, "Come over here, Billy! Look what I've found." On a tilted headstone was the name 'Randall.' Removing the moss as best they could, they could finally read the date. The date read 1740, and the name was "William Randall." On the headstone was also the name of William's wife named Jane and his son named Trever. Going back into town, they inquired about the Randalls at a small restaurant where they had Irish tea and fresh baked scones. The owner was so helpful, and explained there were many Randalls in this area of Antrim. "Mostly well to do farmers. There is a William Randall about 7 miles north of here. That would be a good place to start." Billy tipped his cowboy hat and said, "thanks so much for your help." "By the way," Sandra asked Billy, "Why do you tip your hat?" Billy laughed, and said, "It's a gesture of being polite. My mother told me to be polite before I left." "You are arrogant," Sandra said, "but so far you have been a gentleman to me. That grows on me like moss on the headstones in the cemetery we just visited. It's hard to remove." Sandra laughed and gave Billy a warm hug.

Driving along the road that runs beside the river Bann, they came across the Randall farm. There were cattle in the fields and also sheep. Other fields were bare and empty, since it was about two weeks away from ploughing time. Up to the front door of the old farm house, Billy and Sandra went. The house was large and well kept up. The lawns were manicured to perfection. Ringing the doorbell just once, footsteps were heard approaching the front door. Slowly the door opened, and there stood an attractive middle age woman. "What can I help you with?" she said with a smile. Billy cleared his throat and said, "I'm Billy Randall from Texas, and I'm here in Ireland in search of my ancestor roots." "Please come in." The old farmhouse was remodeled inside, and looked stunning. Mrs. Randall went on to say, "please sit down at the kitchen table, and I will make you some tea. I just made some hot Irish soda bread. Help yourself, and take some Antrim cheese as well." "Thank you for your hospitality, Mrs. Randall. I'm excited to learn more about my ancestor roots. Mrs. Randall smiled as she served the hot tea and soda bread, which was done with perfection. She went on to say while still standing, "my husband will be in from the barn soon. He's attending to a sick cow right now. He knows the Randall history very well." In about ten minutes, the door opened, and Mr. Randall came inside. With a kind voice, Mrs. Randall yelled, "Don't forget to take your barn boots off, William." Coming into the kitchen in his socks, Mr. Randall sees Billy and Sandra at the table. "Oh, we have guests, I see. That's wonderful. Allow me to introduce myself." Billy explained who he was and introduced Sandra as well. Mr. Randall said, "We Randalls have records of two sons born to a William Randall. One was James, and the other William, and they immigrated to the Carolinas in the late1700s. We're not sure of the exact date." Billy spoke up, "My father can trace my roots to that area." Billy was so excited as if he had won a rodeo contest. Mr. Randall then said, "Let me go to the old Prespyterian Church. They have many old records. I'm almost sure we're related." With much research, Mr. Randall found out they were from the same family tree.

In the meantime, he wanted Billy to stay and enjoy his visit to Ulster. Billy was beyond being attracted to Sandra, and Sandra felt the same way. Billy then said to Sandra, "Please visit me on your day off." Sandra replied, "Gladly! I'll look forward to my day off." Sandra said goodbye, and drove back to Belfast. Of course, she had Billy on her mind all the time. Mr. Randall then said to Billy, "would you like to stay and work on our farm for a while? You can get to know how we Irish farm." "Yes, I'd love to stay, and maybe I could even teach you some modern farming techniques," Billy said. "Maybe you could, Billy," Mr. Randall said, "But there is more to farming than what you've learned. There is a practical side to farming." Billy said, "you're like my father - that's what he tries to drill into my head all the time. My father is a good man, but I believe I have an edge on him." Mr. Randall smiled and said, "We will see what you know, I guess. Don't forget: Experience is the best teacher." "When do I start working?" Billy asked. "I'm ready, Mr. Randall. A Texan always has a edge on everything in life." "You have a bit of a know it all attitude, and we will see how you perform over the next few months. We will start ploughing next week, getting 100 acres ready for growing rye, which is exported to Scotland to make whiskey. We have a contract. Do you even know how to plough, Billy?" "Of course I do. We grow some vegetables for our own use on the ranch. I could drive a tractor through the eye of a needle." "Well, in that case, there's a ploughing contest in north antrim next week. I will pay the fee for you to enter." Mr. Randall smiled as he said these words.

Arriving at the Hamilton's farm in north antrim, Billy was ready to show these farmers Texas style ability and everything to do with farming. The tractors on the ploughs were ready, and there were about 100 competitors from all over Ireland. There were 10 tractors and ploughs supplied by the promoters, and there were also old time ploughs and horses. Billy Randall's name was called out, and the announcer said, "We have a young man from Texas who wants to show us the Texas way of doing farming. You will be judged on how even you keep the depth of the furrow. An even depth is important. Above all, how straight the furrow is. There is a white marker at the end of the field, so good luck Mr. Randall." The Irish farmers gave Billy a big cheer, and hand clapping was loud and clear. Billy remarked to those standing by: "This field is what we call a garden in Texas, it's so small." Billy got on the tractor, lowered the plough to the required depth, and off he went down the field. The ground was so wet, and Billy was not quite sure how much throttle to give the tractor. He had a hard time keeping the wheels straight. The marker at the bottom of the field seemed a long ways off. The furrow he was making looked like the trail of a snake -- in and out -- all the way down the field. The spectators were laughing, and urging Billy to go on. Billy was saying to himself, "I'm glad my father is not here. I would be embarrassed to say the least." Billy was way off target, and had to swivel to the right to get close to the marker. He got an ovation from the farmers, and four of them even lifted Billy up on their shoulders. They said, "Thank you from coming all the way from Texas, and showing us the Texas way to plough!" Riding back in the Randalls' car, Billy begged Mr. Randall to not mention the ordeal to Sandra. "I can't do that, Billy. Sandra needs to know your shortcomings as well as your good traits.

The following Monday, the two farm hands ploughed up a 1 acre patch to put in some potatoes. When the acre was ready, Mr. Randall said to Billy, "We're going to plant the potatoes by hand. You can do that." "You don't have to show me what to do," Billy replied. He had never planted potato seeds in his life. After about an hour, Mr. Randall came by to check up on Billy. On seed potatoes, you have to leave about a space of 9 inches to a foot in length, so that the young potatoes have enough room to grow. The side with the most buds should be planted facing upwards. It was a disaster, and Billy had no idea about the buds on the seed potatoes. Looking at Billy with a smile, Mr. Randall said in a firm voice, "Young man. This won't cut it. You will have to replant what you've already done. Do you understand?" "Yes, sir. I hear you, and I will do it over to please you. I'm mad at myself because I didn't ask you first. My father was right, I do need practical experience as well as book knowledge."

It was Tuesday morning the following week and as Billy was going to work, he noticed a stray goat with large horns on the driveway leading up to the family farmhouse. Going back inside, he told Mr. Randall about the goat being loose. "We need to get him back in the pasture right away," said Mr. Randall. "That's not a problem," Billy answered back. "I will make a lariat out of a piece of rope and put it over his horns, the Texas way. This is one thing I'm an expert at, Mr. Randall. Please come out and watch. You will see a Texas cowboy in action." Billy went out to the barn, and found some rope and made a homemade lariat. Approaching the goat, he got within the distance he needed to be, and like a true Texas cowboy, he lassoed the goat. The goat became upset as Bill pulled on the rope to bring him back into the pasture. Putting his head down, the goat charged at Billy and butted him in his stomach, knocking him into a ditch full of nettles and wild rose thorns. By this time, the two hired hands had come by to see what was going on. Mr. Randall was laughing so hard that tears were coming down his cheeks. Then he said to Billy, "Is this the Texas way of herding?" It seems obvious it didn't work. Having dinner that night, Billy confessed to Mr. Randall that he had made a fool of himself, and asked for Mr. Randall's forgiveness. Sandra arrived at the Randall's farm early and was excited to see Billy and the rest of the family. The first thing she said, "How is my Texas boy doing? I'm so glad to see you! I've been telling everyone what a nice young man you are, and my parents as well as all my friends want to meet you." Billy then replied, "I'm so glad you made it out here. I love the farm, the Randalls, and the Irish people. I just feel at home. Mr. Randall gave me the day off, and I was thinking of renting some canoes, and going for a trip down the river Bann. Would you enjoy that, Sandra?" "Yes, I would enjoy that," Sandra said.

They rented two canoes and started canoeing down the Bann. The water was clear and the fields were green, the scenery was beyond being beautiful, and the atmosphere was tranquil and peaceful. After about an hour, they both pulled to the bank, and tied their canoes to a small tree so that the current would not take them down stream. Sandra had brought with her Irish scones and hot tea, and a flask of coffee for Billy. She also brought a blanket to put on the ground while they were having tea and scones. Sitting beside Sandra, Billy asked her, "Do you mind if I put my arms around you?" "I was hoping you'd ask," said Sandra. Sandra laughed, and then said, "Would you think it forward of me if I softly kissed your lips?" But before Sandra kissed Billy, she looked him in the eyes and said, "I've never wanted to be with a man as much as I want to be with you." Then Sandra kissed Billy. Billy responded with soft kisses and a warm hug. The romance had begun in a serious way.

Billy worked through the spring and the summer, and enjoyed himself in every way possible. The two hired hands, Mr. and Mrs. Randall, and the whole neighborhood loved Billy and enjoyed his company. By the end of the summer, Billy and Sandra were deeply in love, so much so that Billy asked Sandra to marry him. "It's about time you asked me, you big Texas boy. I'm so much in love with you, I can't describe it fully." Billy then said, "My folks would love you! You are perfect, Sandra!On a scale of one to ten, you span the big Texas mile." "What's a Texas mile?" Sandra asked. Billy replied, "It is an extended mile, so in other words, you go beyond ten." Sandra had one more year at the university, and would complete that, and then they would get married and live in Texas.

Sandra often said, "I want to work on the ranch, and wear one of those funny hats like you." One evening while out for a stroll, Sandra said, "I fell in love with your hat first, and then you." Laughing, she continued to say, "I'm just putting you on." She then gave Billy a loving kiss and a hug.

THE. TEXAN

In Excess

President Grant
was of Scotch-Irish descent,
and more than one sip of whiskey,
he was known to take.

Before he was president,
he was the number one general
in the Union Army.
President Lincoln was confident
of General Grant's ability,
no doubt.

Other generals
in the Union Army,
thought Grants' drinking
was over the top
Somewhat too much.

During a meeting
at the White House,
they expressed their concerns.
Now President Lincoln was reported to have said:
"What can I do for your, gentlemen?"
Polite as usual he was.
The generals complained
about the excessive drinking of General Grant.
President Lincoln was full of wit,
but his answer was concise and clear:
"Find out where General Grant is getting this whiskey,
and I will give a barrel to you all."

The generals got the message
from honest Abe,
a great president whom people admired.

General Grant was not replaced,
and the union of course, won the war.

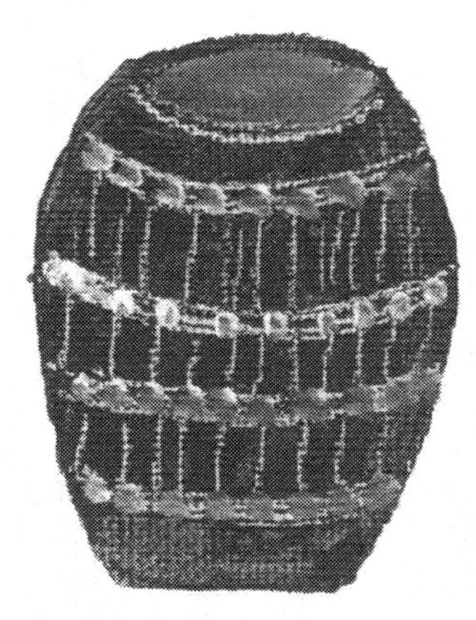

Irish Moss and Lichen

In Ireland
moss and lichen grow
because of dampness,
dew and mist,
you can find it everywhere.
May I use the Irish term:
It has a life of its own.

You come on many shades of green,
light brown and even yellow can be found.
You attach and grow upon exposed rocks
in sluggish riverbeds.

Upon old stone bridges,
you do grow,
and sometimes one has to scrape the stones
to find lime mortar joints,
you are so dense.
Upon the roofs of Irish cottages,
you do grow.
You can be removed,
but next summer you are back again.

We must accept the fact
you are here to stay.
Very seldom you are found
in swift flowing rivers and streams.
Because of the water force,
you don't have time to cling.

Along the rugged Irish coast,
You are found on cliffs,
a mantle of green you do display.
Don't go away.

Please stay.

Old graveyard headstones,
you cover up the names of Irish lords,
and kings, poets, scholars,
and those of hate and fame.

The rain, the sun, the damp atmosphere,
the mist, the dew,
may it feed your roots.
For you had a purpose to grow
in this lonely island we call "Our Land."

The Fishing Leprechaun

Paddy liked to fish in the rivers and streams,
and that for small trout.
His home was in a hollow oak tree,
and outside his rustic bark door was a sign,
"fresh fish for sale and fine Leprechaun wine."
Now his skills in fishing were known all over Ireland.
But he was an arrogant little fellow
and about fishing,
he would brag and boast.

Now at Leprechaun gatherings,
he would brag about his skills,
and then have the nerve with his wine glass
to offer himself a toast.

There were six other wee Leprechauns
that wanted to learn how to fish.
"I will take you to the river and teach you my skills,
and to the head of the colony I will send him a bill.
And only pure gold will be acceptable to me."

Paddy took his gold fishing hooks,
his rod, and his bait.
"Let's get going before it is too late."
He stood on the bank in his little green suit,
and his attitude was as pompous as could be.
He threw his line out while the six little leprechauns watched.
The ripples from the swift current took the bait down stream.
A huge trout took the bait,
and it pulled Paddy right in.
Now Paddy started to yell and scream,
"I can't swim."

"We will pull you out if the rest of our lesson is free."
To this Paddy replied, "it's a deal."

So they took small twig from a huge willow tree,
and they pulled a scared little Paddy to shore.

"Thank you so much, you have saved my life,
let us go back home and there to celebrate
we will have Leprechaun wine and fresh mushrooms,
and we will go back to the river the next full moon."

The Last Visit

The last visit is based on a true story. The names have been changed, so that it will cause no offense to the children and grandchildren that might still be alive.

Mary O'Riley lived in a small cottage in the county of Antrim. The locals called it South Antrim. The terrain was flat with small ponds, peat bogs, and tiny sluggish streams. A short distance from Mary's cottage was her childhood friend's cottage, that of Kathy McVays. Mary and Kathy made a vow that they would visit each other at least once a week. It was a Thursday afternoon around three when Mary dropped in for a visit, and a cup of hot tea.The visit lasted about one hour, consisting of local gossip. Mary got up from the chair with a smile and a glance at Kathy. Then Mary said these words: "Dead or alive, I will be back next week around the same time."

The following Monday, for some unknown reason, Mary passed away. It was a shock to all since she seemed in good health. When Kathy heard about Mary's death, her remarks were, "Oh, I wonder what caused Mary's clock to stop ticking. Poor wee Mary, my best friend." The funeral arrangements were made, and it was decided that Father Boyle would officiate at the committal service.

It was now Thursday, and the grave had been dug. The women would have the food prepared for lunch or dinner (in some parts of Ireland, they call it "lunch," and still others call it dinner). Years ago in Ireland, women seldom went to the burial site, and this was traditional both in the north and south. Father Boyle prayed in the family home, and the men and lads carried the casket outside. Four of them would carry the casket, and when they got tired, others would take over, given that it was about a mile and a half to the family cemetery.

On the way to the burial site was Mary's friend's cottage, the cottage of the McVays. The rain started coming down and it was so heavy that the men and the lads decided to bring the casket inside until the rain let up. Yes, it was around three and Mary was there at the time she told Kathy her friend, but a sad visit it was.

The Turnip Field

The turnips grew on Paddy Doran's farm, but blight and disease had destroyed his potato crop.

It was 1845 and the starving Irish would eat almost anything to stay alive.The turnips were raised for cattle feed,even the sheep at times.Turnip leaves they would eat. At night by candle light, Paddy would look out through the kitchen window, and to see hungry people steal his crops.

He was thankful that he had food to eat, and he would not stop hungry people from seeking a morsel to eat, and bags of oats and barley from a previous harvest, he would give away.One morning he noticed a horse and cart at the end of one of his fields, a nearby farmer named John Clark was taking advantage of Mr. Doran's bumper turnip crop.

Down the field, Paddy went and approached John and told him to leave the field at once. John Clark replied, "Don't you know by the droves, people come by at night and are stealing your crop. Mr. Doran replied, "I see them every night by candle light, and I don't care if they steal my turnip crop, if it means they stay alive. Remove my turnips from your cart and out of this field with your horse and cart, since you have plenty to eat, and why don't you also have mercy on our starving race?"

May the Truth be Known

I know a man. He worked for me for about one year. He told his wife, "I'm going fishing for trout," but that was an excuse. He had a date with a young blonde. He came home, put the trout in the sink for his wife to clean and prepare for the evening meal. But out of the mouth of one of the trout came a blue and white label which read "product of Japan."

Steve, her husband, had gone to the supermarket and bought the trout. He had little time for fishing that day. Her temper flared up and I can understand why. Taking a pan full of trout, and fins and heads and tails, she slowly approached her husband from behind. Steve was on the carpet with a pillow behind his head, watching his favorite show on television. Bonnie took the pan with everything in it and she poured it over his head. They didn't have fish for supper that night. Steve had the shock of his life, and deserved all he got.

Bonnie had enough of Steve -- she filed for divorce, and the marriage ended like that. She raised four children, and did a good job. Some of them were successful as could be. But Steve will always remember his supper that night. Yes, he had the fish poured all over his head -- for out of the mouth of the trout the truth became known.

The Will

It was around midnight when John Doran woke up out of his sleep -- a very deep sleep indeed. He had a strange dream that he died and went to heaven. But before John could enter the gates of heaven, a piece of blank paper stared him in the face. Then he remember that he still needed to make out a will. John thought to himself, "I'm getting older, and death is just around the corner." He turned to his wife, Mary, and gently shook her on the shoulder. Mary, in a grumpy voice, said, "what's the matter with you, John? It's not even the wee hours of the morning yet. Why are you waking me up? The rooster won't be crowing for another five hours." The rooster's name was Mayo, after the county in which they lived. "Mary, we never made a will, and I had a dream that I passed away." Mary replied with a chuckle, "did you go to heaven or to the devil down below?" "Be serious, Mary! We need to make out a will, and after having that dream, I know the time is now," John worriedly said.

Making out a will meant including their three children and two grandsons. Billy, the youngest child, was forty years old, and lived on the family farm with his wife and two children. His children were called Randy and Paul, ages ten and eight. William, the oldest son, was shiftless and lazy, and had little desire to work. Mary often said that if you hid William's food under his work clothes, he'd starve to death. Any money he earned was from part-time work at the local pub. John would say that William is the pub's best customer. But, if you were to compare John's drinking habits with that of his sons, it would be a pretty close call. Tommy, the middle son, had gone into the priesthood at an early age. He'd often tell his father, "I want no part of earthly goods. I just want to serve God, whom I love."

It was still early in the morning, but after drinking a big cup of Earl Grey tea, Mary returned to the kitchen and brought back some paper along with a pen and ink. John started writing: "To Tommy, our middle son, we give you our farm to work as long as there's breath in your body, and the right to stay in our family home for as long as you want. To Billy, we leave our three plough horses along with the sheep and cattle as well as our mean Billy goat. To our only grandsons, we leave the seventy acres of land with the exception of one acre. They will inherit the land after Billy passes away." Mary started to sob as John held her close to him. "To William, our oldest son, we leave an acre down by the trout stream, with the right to an easement to the main road." Mary, with a higher tone of voice, then said, "John Doran, you will sign this will now, for if you have anymore to drink, it will quickly become illegible." John laughed, and said, "you're a fine woman, Mary Doran." Mary answered back, "I love you, John more than a thousand sunsets over Galway Bay."

Now that John Doran's mind was at ease, perhaps his next dream would be about having a cold pint of stout at the local pub, or maybe a second and possibly a third.

The Carpenter

Paddy Logan was not your average carpenter -- he was one of the best. He had a dispute with his boss over his wages in the small town of Dundolk, which is about forty miles north of Dublin.Paddy was sick of receiving low wages for the quality of skills that he possessed. “I’m off to England,” he told his father, and off to Leeds in the County of Yorkshire he went.

He had enough money to rent a small flat in the Irish section of Leeds. Paddy had somewhat of an attitude against the English because they occupied Northern Ireland, and at times his attitude would boil over to the breaking point. With the help of a few pints, Paddy always wanted to fight. He was a typical Irishman! Because of Paddy’s extensive skills, finding a job was as easy as pie. He was hired on as a foreman for a Scottish company that was building a factory in Leeds.

Paddy was a tough boss, and oversaw thirty men. He hired and fired, but never discriminated against a working man’s nationality. For two years Paddy worked up to sixty hours a week, and he would send his pound notes to his family to put in the bank. When the factory was finally finished, Paddy was given a bonus for a job well done. Then he said to his men, “Let us go to a pub and celebrate with a few stouts.” A Welshman who frequently came to the pub had his own special stool…or so he thought. Paddy sat down on the Welshman’s stool and he said to the bartender, “don’t ask me to move.” In through the door, the Welshman came. He was small in height, but had heavy shoulders, and looked as strong as an ox. “Get off my stool, you Irish fool,” was the Welshman’s first arrogant remark. “Excuse me little man, there is a chair in the corner and I will buy you a stout. Otherwise, if you insist on sitting on this stool, I’ll open the pub door, and you’ll hit the sidewall so hard, you’ll crack it,” replied Paddy.

The bartender gave both the Welshman and Paddy a glare, and told them to take it outside. They went outside, and immediately began to knock each other down, and rolled on the ground. Then both of them pounced back up, and started all over again. Paddy hit the Welshman with a right uppercut and knocked him out, and then remarked, “I hate to do this since you’re also a Celt!" A policeman was watching the brawl from across the street, and came over to see what started it.

Paddy wasn't in a pleasant mood, and it showed on his face. He told the policeman that this was a personal vendetta, and to mind his own business. Then policeman then got in the big Irishman's face. Paddy had enough and pulled the policeman's helmet down over his face. That was a big mistake. What Paddy had done was considered an assault on a policeman, even though the officer wasn't injured. To make matters worse, two other police officers were riding their rides and saw the whole thing. They immediately arrested Paddy, and locked him up in jail. He'd be brought before the magistrate in about a week.

The week finally arrived. The courthouse was filled to the brim, and Paddy had to wait an hour before it was time for his hearing. The magistrate called out Paddy's name and said, "Mr. Logan, please come to the bench. You are being charged with disorderly conduct and assaulting a policeman. It seems fit for me to give you a heavy fine along with jail time. Maybe that would give you enough time to cool your horrible Irish temper. After you serve your sentence, I want you to get out of my country, and I mean for good. Now, may I have a reply, Mr. Logan?" "I have a reply for you," Paddy said. "It's this: seeing that The Crown occupies the northern part of my country, I think you should get out of my country first, and then I'll get out of yours." Paddy had a good point to argue, but his disrespect towards English folk was wrong. If his mother were in the courthouse, she would've slapped him silly. The courthouse audience started to roar with laughter at Paddy's response. After the laughter died down, the magistrate spoke, and his tone of voice was far from civil, "Mr. Logan, you don't come into my chambers and disrespect me. You give the Irish a bad name. You will pay a hefty fine, plus two months in prison for assault and one month for contempt."

Paddy did the time and paid his fine. He decided to go back to Ireland a few days after he got out of jail. Arriving home, Paddy saw his mother, Caroline, standing outside the front door. Paddy's friends had written letters to his mother, telling her what was going on. His mother wasn't happy. Before

Paddy could say a word, his mother screamed, "Get into the house!" Caroline started speaking, "I didn't raise you to be disrespectful towards anyone. You will write a letter to the magistrate, the policeman and the Welshman showing remorse for what you've done. I will send the letters to the owner of the pub, and he'll see to it that they're delivered into the right hands. Paddy, you will not spend another night under this roof until you do exactly what I say. Also, you'll go to confession tomorrow, and you can take that to the bank." Paddy looked at his mother with tears in his eyes and said, "I love you, mum. I will do all that you say. After all, you did bring me up right, but I've strayed a wee bit. Please forgive me. I have enough money saved up to buy a small farm, and I will build myself a new house. You and father will also have a new home on the farm. It will be a dream cottage."

"I love you, Paddy," Caroline then added, "and so does that little girl up in Newry. Go up soon to see her. Now write the letters and I will make you some fresh Irish soda bread. Yes, you can have some sharp County Kerry cheese with it, then off to bed with you. I'm sure you need a good night's sleep."

The Scoundrel

Frank O'Brien and his wife Kate lived on a small farm in west Tyrone. It was around sixty acres in size. They raised cattle, pigs, and goats. On the twenty acres of good bottom land, they grew potatoes, turnips, and kale. Kale in Ireland is used to feed animals -- not for human consumption. Now, like most Irishmen, Frank had a wee problem with too much drinking, and I don't mean the pure spring water from a hillside spring on the farm.

It was a Friday morning and the family rooster started crowing. He was like an alarm clock -- always on time. Frank was sleeping soundly and never heard a thing. Kate was wide awake and ready for a full day's work on the farm. She shook Frank on the shoulder and said, "wake up. I have things for you to do." Frank didn't blink an eye, and didn't move. "I've had it with you," Kate said aloud, and her temper was rising like a high tide on Lough Foyle.

Kate went into the kitchen, brought back some cold spring water, and poured it all over Frank's face. Frank responded, "what's wrong with you, Kate? Can't a man have a lie in once in a while?" "Not today. You have to go to the fair," Kate screamed. While she was still talking, Kate pulled her husband's legs over the side of the bed and planted his feet firmly on the floor. Then she said, "May I have a word with you, Frank?" Kate pointed her finger straight into Frank's face.If a man pulled that move, he'd be lying on the ground in agony for weeks. Frank had a punch that could knock out a bull. Kate went on to say, "my father left me this farm because I was the only one he could trust to keep the family farm up. Before he went to heaven, he told me to have nothing to do with the O'Brians. The way you are living, the devil wouldn't even want you if you died. You're a scoundrel, and to make matters worse, I'm in love with a scoundrel." With these last words, Kate started to sob. Frank looked up, and in a soft voice said, "If I ever reform, it will be for you, Kate. I'm in love with you, and your hot temper matches your red hair." Frank O'Brian was tough and strong. He was known to have knocked two men out in a pub, and thrown them outside in a heap. But with Kate, he was always soft spoken and would never ever raise a hand to her.

Now the fair was in a small village just south of County Derry line, with his dog Rover and three cattle, Frank headed to the fair. Rover was no special breed -- just a good herding dog, and he kept the cattle in line. Frank sold the cattle for a good price at the fair, and then stuffed the pound notes into his pockets. On the way home, Frank decided to stop at Mullen's Pub, a quaint little pub indeed -- so quaint in fact that it would be fit for the Irish tourist board. In through the door this six-foot-three-inch man went.His shoulders almost touched the door frame on either side.

Frank slammed his hand down on the bar, and said, "Give me a pint, please, and make sure you pour it with a bartender's skill." At the end of the bar, a man was speaking with an English accent. Frank sat his pint down, and gave the Englishman a giant smile. "Could I buy you another pint, sir?" Frank asked. "Please sit down beside me - I'd like a nice chat." They talked about everything until it was getting late and dark outside. Frank pulled out his pocket watch and said, "I've got to get going now." Frank had an anxious look on his face -- he was afraid of his wife's wrath if he got home too late.

On the way home, he kept on saying to himself, "I'm in big trouble with Kate." Frank wasn't afraid of anyone, except for Kate and her tongue-lashing. He was home at last, and stepped through the door. Frank's head hung low and he looked at the ground in shame and fear. But to Frank's surprise, Kate was very emotional. She began crying and put her arms around him, and after a while, said, "Frank, you need help." Tear drops were falling on Kate's arms. Frank loved Kate dearly, and knew he had to change -- and soon.

Kate spoke, "I will make arrangements for you to see Father Kelly while you are fishing for pike under the bridge that crosses the Foyle. I don't understand why you won't have anything to do with the parish -- you don't even go to mass." Frank replied, "Kate, I can't look Father Kelly in the face. I'm a scoundrel. He'd let me have it." "You are wrong about Father Kelly," Kate said," You can see he has the love of God on his face. He's a good man." The tone quickly changed, and Kate said, "Get the money out of your pocket, Frank. Not one more penny will be spent on stout." Frank didn't utter a word, and he quickly handed over the rest of his pound notes. He knew better.

The following Saturday morning, Frank arrived at the bridge, took out his rod, and baited the fishing hook with sheep liver. With a glance to the side, Frank noted Father Kelly coming down the road. Frank was shaking in his shoes. Father Kelly, with a giant smile on his face, said, “Thank you, Frank, for inviting me into your company.” Frank replied, “I’m a bit of a sinner. I drink and fight, and Kate has to do most of the work on the farm.” With his head bent low, Frank’s last words were, “I’m a scoundrel.” Father Kelly answered back in a soft, comforting voice, “We are all sinners. That’s why Christ died for us, and he took our sins upon himself. God forgives us through him.” Father Kelly then changed the subject: “How is the fishing? Have you caught the fish that’s eluded you for weeks? Kate says you’re determined to catch it at all costs.” Frank answered, “It has eluded me. Would you please pray that I finally catch it? If I catch it, I promise I’ll go as straight as an arrow.” Father Kelly seemed disappointed and said, “I won’t do that. You can’t ask God for things, expecting things or favors in return. But I’ll tell you what -- I’ll catch that big pike for you. I promise, and all I ask for in return is to be able to sit down with you and talk to you about your problems.”

“Oh, Father, if you catch that fish for me, I promise I’ll listen to you until the Irish Sea runs dry. Kate was right -- you are a good man. All the people in West Tyrone love you; even the orange Protestants love you. They think you are a saint,” said Frank. Father Kelly laughed, “I’m no saint, Frank. I have sinned like you, but Christ has forgiven me time after time. Let me go back to the parish and I will bring a special bait back, and I will catch that pike!” After an hour or so, Father Kelly returned with bait, fishing gear, and all. Frank then asked, “What is in your bait? You’ve won contest after contest, and you are known throughout Ireland for your skills. You are famous!” Father Kelly uttered, “I can’t tell you, Frank. It is a secret my father, an ardent fisherman himself, passed down to me.” With the moves of a professional, Father Kelly landed the bait under the shade of a large oak tree on the other side of the river. In less than a minute, the huge fish broke the surface. It took the bait, and the fishing rod bent like a bow. “He is hooked,” Frank said enthusiastically. Father Kelly remained calm, and half an hour later, he finally reeled the fish completely in. Frank asked, "What should we do with the fish? It could feed an army!" Father Kelly replied, "I want to release it. If it's too long out of water, it'll die -- kind of like a man's soul without God. That's why everything needs a source of life, and God is the life source for our souls." With both of his hands on Frank's shoulders, Father Kelly started to pray for Frank, and asked God to give him another chance in life. Frank felt a sense of peace overcome him -- like nothing he'd ever experienced before. He was overjoyed. They both said goodbye to one another, and Frank promised that he'd be at mass next Sunday, and he'd walk a straight line from now on.

Frank finally made it home, and put his arms around Kate as soon as he walked through the door. He proclaimed, "no more fighting, drinking or being a scoundrel from now on. I will love you forever, Kate O'Brian. I promise to work harder, too!" Kate smiled, kissed him, and said, "I'll love you forever, too! I've got a surprise for you as well! I went to the doctor today, and I'm four months along." Frank was stunned and said, "If it's a boy, don't call him Frank. Frank is a scoundrel's name." Kate said, "But why not? You can reform, and Frank will no longer be a scoundrel's name, then. With God's help, Father Kelly's support, and the love of your redheaded wife, we can all do it together. My father was wrong about you -- with me, you are a soft, gentle saint. Now sit down, and I will make you some hot Irish soda bread, but the stout is out."

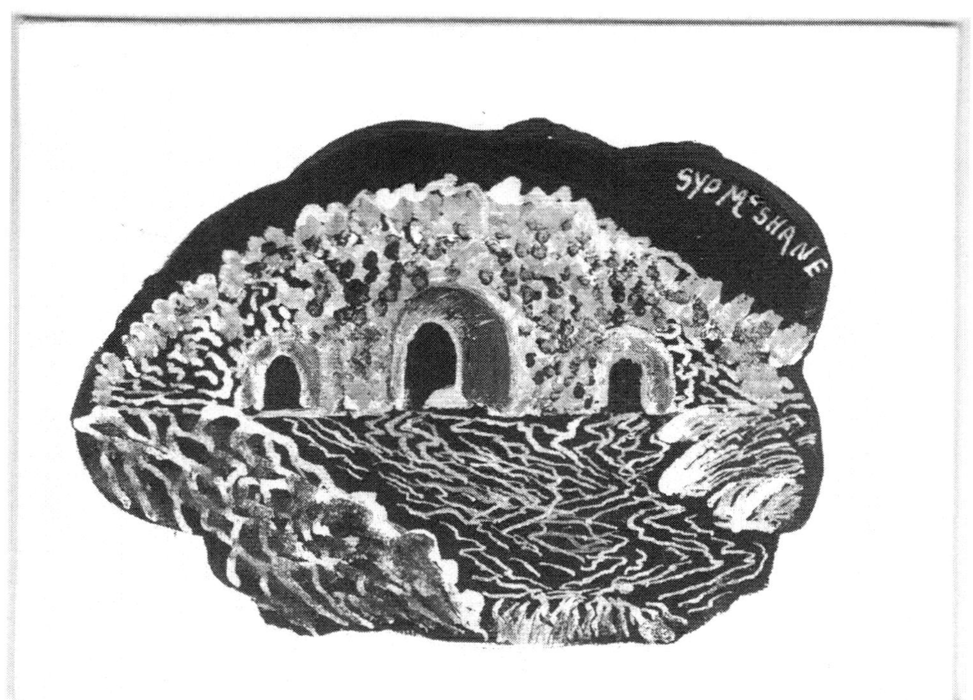
SYD McSHANE

The Stranger

Donegal can be harsh in the winter time and into early spring. The farms are small in comparison with the rest of Ireland. The farm of the O'Hara's was larger than most with around seventy acres. But much of it was only good for sheep. About thirty acres were for crops, barley, wheat and kale for the sheep. In addition about two acres of sandy soil grew great potatoes. Because of weather conditions last year's harvest was poor, but the O'Haras believed God would provide and answer their prayers for a good harvest this year. It was a Friday night and their three children had just gone off to bed. Sean and Mary O'Hara were sitting around the fireplace drinking some hot Irish black tea. With the tea were buttermilk scones. The spread was homemade butter topped off with wild blackberry jam. Sean and Mary loved the land and farming was their way of life. Mary started speaking in a soft, sweet voice and said "I hope we have a better harvest this year. We will be in ruin if we don't. Let us pray that God will be merciful to us. We need his help."

Heads bowed and holding hands, they prayed for about ten minutes. It was now getting late and it was time for some rest. All of a sudden there came a loud knock on the door, then six more with a total of seven. "Let me light a candle" Sean said to Mary. "I must see who it is."

Opening the door he saw a tall man who was clean shaven, but his cloths looked worn out and so did his shoes. The stranger spoke and said "Can I come in for some warmth before I journey on?" "Please come in and you won't have to journey on, in this cold night. There is soft hay in the barn and I will get you wool blankets to keep your warm."

The stranger came in and sat down in a chair beside the fire. Mary brought him some piping hot tea and made some oatmeal with milk and fresh farm cream to pour on top.

"What is your name?" Sean then asked. In a soft voice the stranger's reply was "I'm just a stranger passing through. You will find out I promise you some day. May I have some hot water to wash my feet and a damp cloth to wash my face?" Mary brought a small basin and placed it beside his feet and with it a damp warm cloth to wash his face. Sean went on to say "Mary just knitted a pair of new socks out of Donegal wool and I have an extra pair of shoes. Please take them, for the ones you now have seem to be worn out." There were tears in the stranger's eyes, but they were tears of joy and not of sadness. Then the stranger asked a strange question. "What are you going to plant this year? I need to know. I have a reason for asking this." Mary replied "some barley, wheat and oats plus two acres of potatoes of course." Looking at Sean and Mary with perfect eye contact the stranger smiled and said "there are certain days you must plant and sow. Not before or after these dates. Come harvest time you will believe what I told you is true." Mary took a pen and started writing the dates down. The stranger gave them a date to sow each grain and to plant the potatoes as well. He bade them good night and went out to the barn. As he went there seemed to be a halo of light around his head.

About six in the morning Sean went out to the barn and he noticed the stranger was cleaning the plow. It was so clean it looked like new. "I'm helping you to get ready to plow and then I will be on my way." You don't have to do that. Mary and I did what we had to do and we don't want a reward for it in return". "

"I wanted to do this for you for the kindness you have shown to me, a total stranger just passing through." After a home cooked meal and a hard days' work the strange then said "will you both go out with me to the fields? I want to see where you are going to sow and plant. My visit to the O'Hara farm was not by chance."

Sean was stunned and said "how do you know our last name? I introduced myself as Sean and my wife as Mary." The stranger smiled and said "I know more about the O'Haras than you think and can we leave it at that." Together they all walked out to the fields and chatted as they went. Approaching an old oak tree on the corner of one of the fields the stranger stopped, looked up into the sky hands raised above his head. He spoke in a language that seemed angelic at best. With his hand outstretched he then said thanks again and down the lane and over the hill he went.

The planting and seeding went well and the O'Haras followed the instructions of the stranger to the very day that he told them to seed and plant. Come harvest time there was a bumper crop. It was the best yield the farm ever had. It was triple the average yield. The farmers around the area were amazed at the size of the crop.

Having some tea one evening after the harvest was in Mary looked at Sean and said "I believe that stranger was an angel. He said we would know some day."

The Proposals

Now, Dan Malone was getting up in years. He was around sixty or slightly more. He had one son and a daughter plus his wife Susan. The daughter's name was Brenda and the son was named after his father, but the locals called him young Dan.

His daughter Brenda went to England the age of eighteen and within three months fell in love with a young English man whose name was Robert. Brenda was excited as could be, but then said to Robert "before we get married I need you to meet my father. His approval is important to me." She brought him home to Ireland and had a closed door meeting with her father and Robert. Dan shook Robert's hand and gave him a warm hug, then asked him to leave the room in a polite manner saying that he needed to speak to Brenda alone. "You have my approval" Dan said with a smile. He is rich and seems to be a fine English lad."

"Thank you father, I love you so much, but one thing I want to clear up. Robert is rich in more ways than one. He is caring and giving to the needy and poor. May I say my husband to be is rich in his soul."

Young Dan his son worked hard on the family farm from morning to night and he was quite handsome. The girls had it right. So shy he was that he was afraid to ask a young lady out for a date. But about three miles away in the small town of Athlone there was a young lady called Mary Mc Cray who worked at the local bank. Mary would say to her coworkers "I'm going to ask Dan out on a date and I want to marry him some day."

Down on the stream on the family farm Dan fished for trout after a hard day's work on the family farm. He often said it relaxed him. He also enjoyed eating his catch. Going home from work Mary decided to go by the Malone farm as she could not get Dan off her mind morning, noon and night. All her thoughts were about Dan.

Parking her bike at the old stone bridge she walked casually up a small path to see if Dan was there. To her delight he was. Heart fluttering, she approached Dan with a smile. Her beautiful red hair was slightly over her face. Dan looked up and dropped his fly rod to the ground upon seeing this lovely lady. This was more important than fishing for trout. Dan spoke in a shy soft voice and said "I glance at you all the time when I go into the bank and I mean all the time". Mary smiled and said that his glances didn't go unnoticed. Mary came close and said "may I kiss you on the cheek? You are so handsome, so strong and I am attracted to you like a magnet."

Dan put his hands on Mary's shoulders and looked into her light blue eyes and said "Mary, your beauty is beyond any other lady I have ever seen. There is no one to compare with you in Dublin or Belfast. You are a perfect Irish lass." Dan decided to give Mary a ring. Fishing for trout down on the stream his thoughts were running wild.

Should I ask Mary to marry me down by the water fall or while having tea at the family farm or, maybe I should ask at the family gravesite where the Malone family has six plots. On a Sunday afternoon, after a family dinner at the Malone farm, Dan asked Mary to go for a walk. Mary answered and said "let us go down by the stream, pass the waterfall and then on to the cemetery to pay our respects to your grandparents." The young couple in love while holding hands walked down by the stream stopping now and then to pick wild flowers. They arrived there and stood by Dan's grandparents' grave.

Dan put his arms around Mary's waist and brushed back her red hair so that he could look into her eyes. He softly kissed her lips and with a tear in his eyes said "Mary someday would you like to be buried here with my folks?" This was an Irishman's way of saying that he wanted her to be part of the Malone family. Mary's eyes were wide open. This took him by surprise and when she came to herself she threw her arms around Dan's neck and almost pulled him to the ground. "Yes I want to be a Malone and be married to you and have five other wee Malones just like you."

The Mailman

Years ago in the rural areas of Ireland mail delivery was slow. You walked or had a bike for deliveries. A large leather bag with a flap kept the mail from getting wet. The average route was about nine miles on a round trip. The mail could be delivered in about six or seven hours providing you did not stop to talk or chat which is a trait that the Irish are known for.

For Billy Walker it took him the whole day and into the early evening due to partaking of too many scones or soda bread with tea at more than one house. Billy was a good looking man in his late twenties with red hair, blue eyes and a perfect Irish smile.

The rural school, which was about three miles from Lurgan in the county of Armagh, had an opening for a teacher. The reason for this was that the head master had passed away. A young lady from Scotland applied for the position and within two weeks she was hired. She lived in Belfast and she would drive her car to school every day. One day, Billy while on his route had to bring a letter to the school. He knocked on the country school door and what a surprise was in store for him. A beautiful young lady with blond hair stood there in front of him. Billy gasped and the letter fell to the ground. The young lady started to speak and said "I am Heather Steward and I am from Inverness Scotland." In a nervous tone of voice Billy said "I'm Billy Walker the local mailman and I welcome you to the school Ms. Stewart." "Please just call me Heather. I feel more comfortable with that. I am the proud daughter of a herring fisherman and I have spent many summers on my father's trawler on the North Sea." Heather went on to say that they were having a social event to welcome her here to teach. Then with a smile Heather asked Billy if he would like to come to the event. "I would love to come" Billy replied, and "when is the event?" "It is this Saturday night" Heather replied. "If you don't think I am being forward I will pick you up in my car which my father bought me for my twenty fourth birthday."

"I don't think that is forward at all and I would appreciate that." Heather picked Billy up around six. She was dressed in a plaid skirt which represented the Stewart clan and a highland sweater. "She looks stunning" Billy thought to himself. He had on a tie and shirt and a fine set of clothes.

Heather glanced at Billy and said "you look handsome tonight and I would like to dance with you at least once and into the wee hours of the morning. Please also dance with others if you wish as I am not the jealous type."

The social event went as well as expected and everyone made Heather feel at home and she was delighted. Now Heather only wanted to dance with Billy and she could not keep her eyes off him. The remarks that were going around were about what ever has gotten into Billy as he seemed to be in a different world. No one has ever seen him like this. This must be "love at first sight".

Billy and Heather started seeing each other at least twice a week but during school hours it was all business with Heather as she was devoted to her profession.

The courtship went on for about a year or so and they were falling deeply in love with each other. Walking along Lagan canal one evening with the harvest moon bright and a slight chill in the air, a perfect romantic atmosphere was created for a young couple in love. Billy stopped and turned to face Heather and softly kissed her lips. Heather then gazed into Billy's eyes and said "I'm in love with you Billy Walker and from the first day that I met you I said to myself that this is the only man that I want in my life." Billy stuttered and had a hard time getting words out and all he could say was would you over and over again. Heather started laughing and said "come on out with it now and are the next words after would you are they marry me? "Yes, Billy and make it soon as I am crazy about you. Can we go back to Scotland and have the minister perform the ceremony on my father's trawler, in the harbor with all my family? I also want your family there. Please Billy would you do that for me? Billy with a warm hug said "I would marry you on the top of Mount Everest or in a green Scottish glen beside a rippling trout stream." As Billy continued speaking his eyes filled with warmth. "Let us go by the old school house where I first set my eyes on the most beautiful lass Scotland has ever seen and there in your study we will make our wedding plans."

Heather's father would bring the trawler in from the sea, a Presbyterian minister would officiate as the Stewards were devout Presbyterians.

Heather's only sister would be the maid of honor and a proud father would give her away. Her father thought that Billy was the best choice his daughter could ever make.

The wedding day came and went according to plan. The smell of fish was in the air and the seagulls filled the sky. Other trawlers were pulled a long side the boat as the Stewards were well respected for their honesty and integrity. After they both had taken their solemn wedding vows the happy couple cut the wedding cake which was decorated the colors of purple heather that grows in the highland glens. They had their honeymoon in Galway Ireland in a quaint little cottage in a small cove.

When they came back home a warm welcome awaited them. At the school the children were told that it is no longer Miss Steward but Mrs. Walker.

Billy's life changed for the better now with no more long chats as he delivered the mail forthwith.

He wanted to spend most of his time with Heather and two years later twins were born. The couple named the one boy James after heather's father anc the other boy Steward after heather's maiden name. Heather continued to teach and Bill still delivered the mail but when a letter came to the school heather would open the door and give Billy a smile and say "I love you but I am busy and I do not have time to chat. I am looking forward to having a wonderful evening with you. Again I say I love you Billy".

Copyright

32923399R00091

Made in the USA
San Bernardino, CA
20 April 2016